Maples

Rosemary Barrett

Photographs by Derek Hughes

FIREFLY BOOKS

A FIREFLY BOOK

Published by Firefly Books Ltd. 2004

First published in 2004 in New Zealand by David Bateman Ltd.,
30 Tarndale Grove, Albany, Auckland, New Zealand

First Printing

Publisher Cataloguing-in-Publication Data (U.S.)

Barrett, Rosemary, 1931-
       Maples / Rosemary Barrett ; Derek Hughes, photographer. —1st ed.
[96] p. : col. photos. ; cm.
Includes bibliographical references and index.
Summary: Introductory guide to growing maples, including
hardiness zone information. Provides practical advice on how to
plant, propagate, cultivate and landscape with maples.
ISBN 1-55297-885-0
ISBN 1-55297-884-2 (pbk.)
1. Maple. 2. Trees. I. Hughes, Derek. II. Title.
635.9/77378 21   SB413.M365.B37   2004

National Library of Canada Cataloguing in Publication

Barrett, Rosemary
       Maples / Rosemary Barrett ; photographs by Derek Hughes.
Includes bibliographical references and index.
ISBN 1-55297-885-0 (bound).--ISBN 1-55297-884-2 (pbk.)
       1. Maple. I. Hughes, Derek II. Title.
SB413.M365B37 2004   635.9'77378   C2003-905567-1

Published in the United States in 2004 by
Firefly Books (U.S.) Inc.
P.O. Box 1338, Ellicott Station
Buffalo, New York 14205

Published in Canada in 2004 by
Firefly Books Ltd.
3680 Victoria Park Avenue
Toronto, Ontario M2H 3K1

Printed in China through Colorcraft Ltd., HK

Page 1: *Acer palmatum* varieties planted along a stream bank
Page 2: *Acer palmatum*
Page 3: *Acer palmatum* 'Sango-kaku

For Kathy, Kevin and Peter

Acknowledgments
I gratefully acknowledge Derek Hughes and Ann Bayliss, for without their help this book would not be
possible. My thanks also to my horticultural consultants Bill Robinson and Walter Miller of Rotorua whose
help is greatly appreciated.

Contents

Preface   6

Introduction   7

1. Cultivation   11

2. *Acer palmatum*   19

3. Other Japanese Maples   37

4. Born in North America   43

5. Maples from Other Lands   49

6. Landscaping with Maples   55

7. Companion Planting   65

8. Landscaping with Maples in Containers   83

Epilogue   89

Sources of Maples in North America   94

Bibliography   95

Index   95

Preface

Before starting to write this book I asked myself why I was doing it, and for whom. The answer was this – I love maples above all other trees, and would therefore like more to be grown. If I wrote a book that would tell gardeners who had not grown any (or many) maples before, how very beautiful they are, and how very easy and rewarding they are to cultivate, then I would feel I had provided information that hopefully would mean more maples would be planted.

In their splendid book *The Garden Tree*, Alan Mitchell and Allen Coombes wrote, "A herbaceous garden disappears in two years of neglect, but a tree thrives on 200 years of it." They added: "No one need refrain from planting trees for fear they will not be looked after. They will look better if cared for, but will survive even if they are not."

Planting a tree is a very significant task, not because it is difficult – quite the opposite, in fact – but because it will flourish after the gardener has gone to the great arboretum in the sky, and may survive for dozens, if not hundreds, of years. The seasonal changes will delight succeeding generations as they did the innovative gardener, and wildlife from bugs to birds will take shelter in its branches.

Any book written for gardeners as distinct from a botanical treatise must surely place heavy emphasis on the Japanese maples, *Acer palmatum*, *A. p.* var. *dissectum* and *A. japonicum*, although others will be discussed as well. This emphasis is made because the obvious beauty of Japanese maples has enthralled gardeners for hundreds of years, and also because many are small trees that may be accommodated in any patch that calls itself a garden.

Why are maples so special? They are prized for their wonderfully colored leaves – brilliant in the spring and often more brilliant in the fall – and they have attractive seeds and a graceful habit of growth, whether it be upright or weeping. As the seasons change so does the appearance of the trees, but whatever the changes, they are always beautiful. For me, and I am sure for legions of others, these are trees of perfection.

By growing maples, gardeners will receive great delight from these changing beauties through the endless cycle of seasons. They will be giving posterity pleasure not only by enhancing the landscape, but by improving the environment – and all this from a simple desire to beautify the garden. If you agree with me that maples are some of the most beautiful trees, then let's plant a lot of them.

It is necessary to do some planning before planting, to decide what is to go where, because, although it can be done, it is neither practicable nor desirable to move trees around like perennials. We will discuss this aspect in the chapter on landscaping. In other chapters we will discuss varieties, their requirements and where to place them.

Introduction

Almost all maples are deciduous trees, and they vary greatly in size and shape. They have palmate leaves, which in nonbotanical language means they are shaped like a hand, and you could (with the use of a little imagination) see the points as fingers. These "fingers," or lobes, usually number between five and nine; occasionally 11. Some are deeply cut, and some, just to confuse the issue, are not cut at all, though most of these do not actually concern us, being either unsuitable as garden subjects or not in cultivation.

I imagine that when most of us think of a leaf (except in fall) we most likely think of it as green, but if we think a little longer we realize that this is not always the case. *Acer palmatum* 'Bloodgood' has dark purple leaves; *A. p.* 'Orido-nishiki' is variegated in pink and cream; *A. p.* 'Beni-komachi' is startling scarlet; *A. p.* 'Shin-deshojo' is bright pink; *A. platanoides* 'Crimson King' is a deep, dark red; and *A. pseudoplatanus* 'Brilliantissimum' is shrimp pink. There are many more, of course, which will be discussed in the following chapters.

In fall, maples' leaves are a vibrant glory in red, gold, crimson and orange. It is clear that one of the main reasons for growing maples is their wonderful leaves, never static, changing all through the seasons, and never less than beautiful.

When you think of a Japanese cherry you more than likely visualize a froth of pink blossoms. Maples are not in this league, but many do have pretty

Right: *Acer palmatum* 'Sumi-nagashi'

flowers – not the sort you put in a vase, but attractive all the same. They grow in either racemes or bunches called corymbs. Some maples, such as *Acer japonicum* 'Aconitifolium' and *A.* 'Rubrum', flower before the leaves unfurl. These flowers are beautiful in themselves, adding an appreciated extra dimension to the trees. Others flower as the leaves appear, and are not quite so striking.

Where you have flowers you usually get seeds. Those of maples are gorgeous, for they have two wings each with a seed in the center. These winged seeds are known as keys or samaras, and in *Maples of the World*, authors D.M. van Gelderen, P.C. de Jong and H.J. Oterdoom remark that they "are as much the hallmark of maples as acorns are of oaks." The wings look vaguely like the blades of a helicopter, and help the seed flutter away to find a good place to germinate when ripe.

Maples really are a cornucopia of riches, for many of them have striking bark as well. This is particularly attractive in winter when you are not distracted by flowers, seeds or leaves. The term "snakebark" is applied to those with striped bark – sometimes green and white, sometimes purple with white striations.

It can be easily seen what treasures maples of all sizes and shapes are, and how fortunate we are to have such wonderful choices.

It is always rewarding to know something about the history of the plants we grow, just as most of us like to know something about the people who went before us.

Maples come from the Northern Hemisphere, from the temperate climate of North America and, of course, from China, Japan and Korea. Although various species live close together and are very similar in appearance, they do not interbreed.

The history of plant hunting makes fascinating reading. It is beyond the scope of a book such as this to do any more than note that Britain, Holland, France and North America all had plant hunters, very often missionaries, sending home plants and seeds from various countries, and we have reaped the enormous benefit of their endeavors. In their travels, these plant hunters found maple seeds and plants (as well as thousands of other plant species) that they sent home and these were developed into plants that could be cultivated in gardens.

At the end of a long chain of bravery, endeavor, skill and zeal, we, as present-day gardeners, can reap the benefits of hundreds of superb cultivars in myriad sizes, shapes and colors. We may not often give a thought to the history of the plants in our gardens, but just by growing them we are playing a role in their preservation. However brave and resourceful the plant hunters, and however enthusiastic the connoisseurs, unless we ordinary gardeners grow what has been so laboriously gathered for us, these treasures could well be lost.

Hardiness Zone Map

This map has been prepared to agree with a system of plant hardiness zones that have been accepted as an international standard and range from 1 to 11. It shows the minimum winter temperatures that can be expected on average in different regions.

Where a zone number has been given at the end of an entry, the number corresponds with a zone shown here. That number indicates the coldest areas in which the particular plant is likely to survive through an average winter. Note that these are not necessarily the areas in which it will grow best. Because the zone number refers to the minimum temperatures, a plant given zone 7, for example, will obviously grow perfectly well in zone 8, but not in zone 6. Plants grown in a zone considerably higher than the zone with the minimum winter temperature in which they will survive might well grow but they are likely to behave differently. Note also that some readers may find the numbers a little conservative; we felt it best to err on the side of caution.

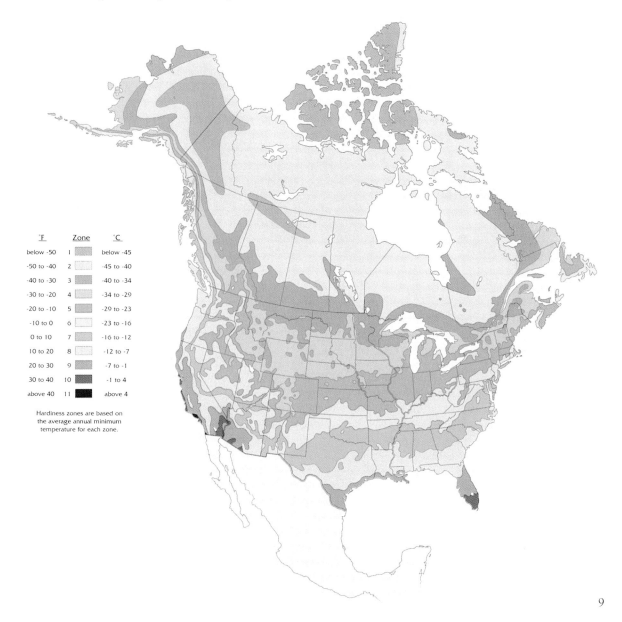

°F	Zone	°C
below -50	1	below -45
-50 to -40	2	-45 to -40
-40 to -30	3	-40 to -34
-30 to -20	4	-34 to -29
-20 to -10	5	-29 to -23
-10 to 0	6	-23 to -16
0 to 10	7	-16 to -12
10 to 20	8	-12 to -7
20 to 30	9	-7 to -1
30 to 40	10	-1 to 4
above 40	11	above 4

Hardiness zones are based on the average annual minimum temperature for each zone.

CHAPTER 1

Cultivation

Trees are very easy – in fact, downright accommodating – to grow. It is axiomatic, however, to say that if more care is taken, better and quicker growth will result. By catering to the specific needs of maples you will increase your chances of raising some outstanding trees.

Soil

Maples are very adaptable, and thus will grow in all types of soil, but most do best in a slightly acidic soil (i.e., between pH 6.5 and pH 5.0). This does not mean that you cannot grow maples if your soil is very alkaline, just that you should take some remedial action such as adding generous amounts of organic matter like compost, leaves and peat moss to buffer the natural pH. Should your soil be impossibly awful (e.g., dry and rocky), do not despair because maples grow very well in containers.

Acers, as with most plants, like a good, loamy, free-draining soil; they will not tolerate wet feet. If you need to improve your soil structure, well-rotted animal manures and compost are excellent additives. It must be emphasized, however, that maples are not too fussy and will grow in a wide range of soil types.

Location

Although they can cope with a wide range of soil types, it cannot be emphasized too often that Japanese maples do not tolerate wind, though many other types of maples can handle windy locations

Opposite: *Acer rubrum* 'Armstrong'

Acer shirasawanum 'Autumn Moon'

to some degree. Generally, maples are not trees for coastal places where salt winds occur. If you have a breezy site it is necessary to find a good sheltered place within your garden where cold winds do not blow. This should not be too difficult in most gardens. Often you will find that there are sheltered microclimates you can take advantage of.

Maples like some sun so don't plant them in shady locations. If you have warm summer temperatures, plant your maples where they will receive full morning sun but dappled shade through the hottest part of the day. In climates with cooler summers, where temperatures do not exceed 90°F (32°C), all-day sun is advisable. If maples don't receive enough sun, they will not die, but they will become spindly and will not color as they should, which is one of

Left: A grouping of Japanese maples
Below left: *Acer palmatum* var. *dissectum*

supplied as bare-root plants and are planted when they are dormant (when there are no leaves). If planting in fall or through winter in cooler climates, you will need to protect the roots from freezing with a deep mulch (kept away from the trunk to avoid any rot problems). Otherwise, wait until the ground thaws and plant as early as possible in the spring. Sometimes maples are supplied potted in containers and are available all year. Again, depending on your climate, you may plant anytime, but planting during summer is not recommended because you will need to be very assiduous about watering. Maples do not like to dry out and their shallow root systems can be susceptible to this.

Once you have chosen a suitable place, as is always suggested, dig a hole bigger than the root-ball – twice as big is ideal – so the roots will not have to struggle through compacted soil. If your soil is predominantly poor-draining clay, dig an even wider hole, as shallow as you can while still burying the rootball, as this gives the roots a good chance of establishing quickly near the surface where they will not be waterlogged.

Once you have dug the hole, put in a lot of organic matter, such as compost, as this is your only chance to get it directly to the roots. You could also add a little fertilizer in the form of slow-release pellets, and in dry climates consider throwing in a handful of water-absorbent crystals. When every-thing is in, put the soil back in the hole and mix thoroughly. Then remove all but the bottom 6 in. (15 cm) of mix.

Take your tree out of its container, loosen the roots gently, and if they are growing in a circle, cut them with a sharp knife so that these roots can change direction and grow downwards. Place the rootball in the prepared hole (at the same level as it was in the container), then fill the hole half full with the soil mix. Water in, shaking the plant gently

their most exciting attributes. Tolerance of, and need for, sun also varies between maples; for example, some variegated and purple leaf maples are happy in sunnier situations, so check specific requirements when buying.

Planting

You can plant maples any time from late fall to early spring, depending on your climate. They are often

Acer buergerianum, the trident maple

so there are no air pockets. Wait until the water has disappeared then fill the hole with the remaining mix. Firm it gently, but do not stamp heavily, as this would only compact the soil. Water lightly. If you still have some mulch left, apply it to the topsoil and feel confident that you have given your tree a great start.

You can stake the tree if it's a tall one, but because of their shrubby growth maples do not usually need this.

After care

For the first year after planting, especially through the summer, it is advisable to check that the soil remains moist. After a year, such vigilance will not be necessary as the tree will have its roots firmly in the soil and ordinary rainfall should suffice. However, if your climate is dry you will need to water regularly. Maples have shallow root systems and so cannot draw water from deep in the soil. Watering with a lawn sprinkler system up to the drip-line (the line around the tree that the leaves reach) is ideal.

Maples, as has been mentioned, are not greedy and, in common with most trees, do not require fertilizer, but if you feel like spoiling them a little, you could apply some slow-release fertilizer in the spring. A top dressing of compost or similar organic matter is splendid, and it would be a good idea to do this once a year since your initial dressing will have broken down. However, you need not do any of this as your tree will grow without coddling – but perhaps it will grow even better with a little fuss.

Mulching is worthy of special mention here as it is important for maples in two specific instances. In warmer climates, mulching in summer will help to preserve moisture and keep the roots cool. Winter mulching is essential in zones 4 and 5 where the ground freezes and heaving can be a problem. Also consider planting your maples in a protected position by a fence or hedge.

Where your climate is more severe, in zones 4 and below, you will need to grow some of the less hardy species in containers and overwinter them in an unheated cold frame, garage or basement. Bring

the containers in when nighttime temperatures drop below 15°F (−10°C) and put them out again in early spring once the ground has thawed. Don't put them in a heated room, as they will need low temperatures to ensure winter dormancy. They won't need light either, but do check to make sure the container's soil is moist.

Pests and diseases

Maples are not much bothered by either pests or diseases as long as their cultivation requirements are met: some sun, good drainage, not too much wind, enough water. The following are some possible hazards, but I must strongly emphasize that other than die-back they are very unlikely to trouble you in a garden situation.

There are the usual insects found on cultivated plants, but maples do not suffer severely from these. Aphids and scale insects can be a problem in early spring, but a spray with a winter dormant oil before leaf buds open is a good precautionary measure if this is a problem in your garden; otherwise, a strong spray with a hose will usually dislodge aphids once they appear.

A common problem in maples is die-back, which especially affects new twigs. Sometimes whole branches can be affected, dying back in the winter. The solution is just to cut off the affected branches and hope the tree survives.

The most likely cause of die-back is something called verticillium wilt, a soil-borne fungus disease with no real cure. If you believe this is the culprit, avoid planting other maples in the same spot. However, if your tree does have some die-back it is much more likely to be something less sinister. Quite often in warmer climates the plant most injudiciously puts on new growth in the late fall that may not have a chance to harden before winter. Just prune the dead branches back to the nearest healthy bud. Another possible cause is root rot, which occurs when the

drainage is not sufficient. This is more common in container-grown maples.

If your maple shows signs of something called chlorosis – an unnatural yellowing of the leaves – it is probably because the site is too wet, soil temperature is too cool or the soil is too alkaline. If you think the cause is a soil deficiency you should have your soil analyzed, but any deficiency will likely affect other plants in your garden.

Having told you about these possibilities I will quote that great American maple expert J.D. Vertrees, who said of maples, "When grown under normal conditions and with good culture, they are remarkably free of disease and insect problems."

Pruning

J.D. Vertrees also wrote: "We are convinced that a major sin in landscaping and gardening is the constant neglect of pruning and shaping our plants." Now it has to be remembered that Mr. Vertrees was steeped in Japanese horticultural lore, and the Japanese have raised pruning to an art form. For the practical gardener the techniques are simple. If your maple is of the upright variety, and if you have allowed it plenty of space, leave it alone other than to remove any dead branches. It you have a weeping maple you will notice that the branches underneath the canopy die for lack of light. This does not show when the plant is in leaf, so after leaf fall remove all these branches, even though you might well have to crawl underneath to accomplish this.

If your maple does not have unlimited space, and you can see that it may grow too large if left unchecked, then judicious pruning is in order. You will need to think ahead so that instead of attacking the tree ruthlessly when it has outgrown its allotted space, you carefully prune and shape it each year so that you have a beautifully proportioned tree, not an unsightly hacked mess that could take years to recover.

If you really need to prune, make sure you have a sharp pruning saw and pruning shears (secateurs).

Opposite: *Acer palmatum* var. *dissectum* 'Ever Red'

Pruning is best done in winter when you can see the tree's structure. Make a clean cut as close as possible to the trunk. Do not use pruning paste as it's now thought to inhibit healing.

Propagation

Perhaps it is my age, or maybe it is my tendency to want it all to happen yesterday, but for whatever reason I prefer my plants tidily encased in a plastic container, all ready to be planted so I can reap their benefits quickly. This is not, I understand, the way everyone regards the matter of growing their own, so you may try the following methods.

Growing from seed

This is the simplest option, but you will not get plants that are true to type if the seeds are from hybrids. If the seeds are from species you will still get variation from the parent. Seed may be the easiest option, especially if you want a lot of trees at little cost, but unfortunately it is not all *that* easy. If the seeds were left to fall upon the ground they would not germinate until they had experienced winter chill. Once you have gathered your maple seeds when ripe in the fall, it is necessary to stratify them. This means you need to place the seeds between layers of moist sand or peat moss in containers in your refrigerator, set at 34–46°F (1–8°C). This stratification period must last for a minimum of 60 days, to a maximum of 120 days. In the spring, after this artificial winter, the seeds will be ready for planting.

Plant the maple seeds as you would any other – that is, in a good seed-raising mix, giving constant attention to moisture, watching out for pests and spraying for damping off (rotting) with a fungicidal spray. When the seedlings are large enough, pot them in individual containers. After a year or three you might find that you have something outstanding; it is more likely that you will have some very pleasant trees, excellent for planting large areas, but very unlikely to be as good as the many named varieties available.

Top: *Acer palmatum atropurpureum* 'Okagami'
Above: *Acer palmatum atropurpureum*

I would not say that you are wasting your time by growing maples from seed, but I do think that what horticulturists and hybridizers have achieved should not be ignored. Years of work have gone into producing stunning plants. I take advantage of this, but you might think differently, so by all means have fun doing it yourself. Just remember, you are not very likely to improve upon what professionals have done, and if you just want a very limited number for your garden, have the best. If you are going to plant a lot of maples, however, growing from seed remains an attractive low-cost option.

Cuttings

To grow maples from cuttings you must have an automatic watering system to keep the cuttings turgid; this is easiest in a conservatory or greenhouse where a moist atmosphere is not a problem. The medium in which the cuttings are placed needs to have very good drainage. These mixes are often peat and sand, or perlite and sand, or one of the professional mixes that you can buy.

For summer cuttings of semihardwood you will need to cut a piece of this year's growth that is about 3–6 in. (8–15 cm) long; strip all but the last pair of leaves, make a slanting cut at the base, dip in rooting hormone and insert into the mix. Bottom heat, supplied by cables under the mix, makes success more certain, and you must keep the cuttings moist at all times. Then you must wait to see if your cuttings root, which will take some months. After they are rooted, pot them, keep them shaded until they have recovered from the shock, then plant them in the vegetable garden until they are large enough to be permanently placed in the garden.

Some varieties propagate from cuttings better than others; the weeping maples (dissectums) are very difficult indeed. Both skill and patience are needed for the production of maples, but where there is a will there is a way. My way is to will a professional to do it.

Grafting and budding

Propagating maples by grafting or budding is probably best left to the professional, but if you

Above: The delicate flowers of *Acer japonicum* 'Aconitifolium'

are serious, you could learn this highly skilled way of producing trees that are exact replicas of the trees that provided the buds. To do this you must first have understocks, which in this case are *Acer palmatum* seedlings.

These seedlings must be grown for from one to three years. Then they must be grafted or budded. To do this it would be necessary to enlist the help of a professional or to buy a very good book and study it assiduously. Good luck!

CHAPTER 2

Acer palmatum

Should you want a small-growing tree that offers gloriously colored leaves in both spring and fall, and is trouble-free and easy to grow, the Japanese maple *Acer palmatum* is an outstanding choice. In the following pages I have divided the maples according to color, choosing what I have found to be the most beautiful and satisfactory. I have also given approximate heights and widths. This is not an exact science, however, as growing conditions and age must be taken into account. In other words, if a tree is 100 years old, it will naturally be very much larger than one that is 15 years old.

The choice in red

Red is a strong color in the garden, and in the plant world the red Japanese maples are truly dramatic. There are a great number in red, but I shall just discuss those with which I am familiar – and that are readily available. This approach will give plenty of scope to gardeners. The true collector or connoisseur may spend a lifetime gathering up the more obscure cultivars, probably by importing from many countries. This does not necessarily mean they will have trees that are more beautiful than the ones that will be discussed, just that they will be different. As with all collections, the fun may be in the search.

Do note that "red" maples are red in the spring and fall, but very often in the summer months the leaves turn a sort of bronze-green color. This I find just splendid, for if you were growing a conifer it

Opposite: *Acer palmatum* 'Katsura' in the background with the red maple 'Beni-komachi' in front

Acer palmatum 'Okagami'

would basically remain an unchanging blob all season. Also, the generic term "red" will encompass leaves that are such a deep color as to be almost purple.

Acer palmatum **'Aratama'**, although small, is strong-growing. Its bright red foliage makes it as striking as a flowering tree. 3 ft. by 3 ft. (1 m by 1 m). ZONES 6–8.

Acer palmatum **atropurpureum** (syn. 'Atropurpureum') is the most common red maple and one of the most highly regarded. It is a very dark red, almost black-red, and unlike many, does not "bronze out" in the summer. In the fall it turns the most brilliant scarlet red, an absolute bonfire. Discussing

Acer palmatum 'Beni-komachi'

height is a tricky business but my 30-year-old tree is about 25 ft. (8 m) tall. It is strong-growing and highly recommended. 25 ft. by 25 ft. (8 m by 8 m). ZONES 6–8.

There are some splendid selections from *Acer palmatum atropurpureum* including one of my top favorites. This really special tree is called 'Okagami'. It is a very dark red in the spring, which you might not think seems so very special – but just wait for the fall. Its brilliant, dazzling scarlet leaves with the sun behind them make for a sight not easily forgotten. The tree is upright to about 12 ft. (4 m), though with age it will be a little taller. 12 ft. by 9 ft. (4 m by 2.7 m). ZONES 6–8.

Three other *Acer palmatum atropurpureum* selections are well worth considering. The first choice is

'Oshio-beni'. Its new growth is orange-red, then reddish green and finally a bright scarlet. 18 ft. by 12 ft. (6 m by 4 m). ZONES 6–8.

The second is 'Moonfire', a fairly new cultivar. Characteristically, its leaves are very dark in the spring, but they do not change in the summer, which is a virtue. In the fall there is a splendid display of crimson. When it is young, the new shoots can grow 3 ft. (1 m) in a season, but growth slows as it ages. 12–15 ft. by 15 ft. (4–5 m by 5 m). ZONES 6–8.

The third selection from *Acer palmatum atropurpureum* that I grow and admire is 'Sumi-nagashi'. Bright red new leaves turn to deep maroon in summer and then to glowing crimson in the fall. As with the other maples mentioned, it is obligingly strong-growing. 12 ft. by 9 ft. (4 m by 2.7 m). ZONES 6–8.

"Beni" means "red" in Japanese and there are a good number of acers with this prefix, many of which are not readily available.

A very beautiful small tree, which I guess could be classified as a large shrub, is 'Beni-fushigi', hailing reasonably recently from the United States, but now becoming more widely available. It is distinguished by the most astonishingly vivid scarlet leaves, and would grace any garden, large or small. 6 ft. by 6 ft. (2 m by 2 m). ZONES 6–8.

'Beni-hime' is very small, with delightful tiny red leaves both in spring and fall. It rejoices in sun and is much hardier than its delicate looks would suggest. 3 ft. by 3 ft. (1 m by 1 m). ZONES 6–8.

'Beni-komachi', if not my very favorite, must be close to it. It is classed as a semidwarf – a very nice garden height. Its little leaves give a lacy effect, making it a treasure I would not be without. The new leaves, which look delicate (but are not),

Acer palmatum

are truly the most astonishing bright crimson – a color to take your breath away. The color darkens during the season and then returns in the fall. It is particularly satisfying to note that this plant was bred by J.D. Vertrees, whose book *Japanese Maples* has been a bible in this household for many years. 6 ft. by 6 ft. (2 m by 2 m). Zones 6–8.

'Beni-maiko' is just as beautiful, with intense red leaves in spring, turning greenish red in summer and scarlet in fall. It would be difficult to choose between it and 'Beni-komachi', so the only solution is to have both. 3 ft. by 3 ft. (1 m by 1 m). Zones 6–8.

I have a little grove of a quite outstanding maple called **'Beni-otake'**. It has two special features. The first is its bamboolike leaves of a good red. The second attribute is that it keeps putting on more leaves of the brilliant spring color, so it is always

Right: *Acer palmatum* 'Beni-fushigi'
Below: *Acer palmatum* 'Beni-otake'

eye-catching, and in the sun it really does glow. Of course, its scarlet fall color is also impressive. 10 ft. by 6 ft. (3 m by 2 m). Zones 6–8.

'Bloodgood' is easily grown, like those already mentioned, and also like them it has large leaves. These leaves are very dark and hold their color until the fall when they turn bright crimson. 'Bloodgood'

Above: *Acer palmatum* 'Fireglow'
Left: *Acer palmatum* 'Bloodgood'
Below left: *Acer palmatum* 'Chishio'

has attractive seeds, which have bright red wings. 15 ft. by 10 ft. (5 m by 3 m). Zones 6–8.

'Burgundy Lace' takes its name from the color of burgundy wine and has very deeply divided leaves, which, conceivably, might remind you of lace. It makes a spreading small tree. Its shape could be most useful as a contrast in a mixed palmatum planting, an idea explored in a later chapter. 12 ft. by 12 ft. (4 m by 4 m). Zones 6–8.

'Chishio' is little, but its brilliant spring colors, scarlet with a tinge of orange, are as arresting as many a larger tree, and its fall color is bright in red and orange. It is good in a container. 10 ft. by 6 ft. (3 m by 2 m). Zones 6–8.

'Fireglow' is much like the popular 'Bloodgood'. Some people think it is better, but I think the two complement each other nicely. 'Fireglow' has the same dark red leaves – scarlet in fall – but is a little smaller growing and possibly a neater shape. 9 ft. by 6 ft. (2.7 m by 2 m). Zones 6–8.

'Inazuma' is sometimes called the thunder maple – if ever there was an obscure name this must be it. The leaves are a dark purple-red, then green, which perhaps sounds reasonably ordinary, but wait till you see the fall color, which is bright red-crimson, considered one of most spectacular selections. When you consider the wonderful fall colors of *Acer palmatum* generally, this is very high praise indeed. 30 ft. by 20 ft. (9 m by 6 m). ZONES 6–8.

'Pixie' is accurately named, for it is very small. The purple-red spring leaves turn scarlet in the fall. It is a very useful maple for small gardens, rock gardens or growing in containers. 3 ft. by 3ft. (1 m by 1 m). ZONES 6–8.

'Red Pygmy' is not, in my opinion, so very small, because it grows to about 6 ft. (2 m). It is named for its beautiful spring color – dark red. It makes a nice change in the fall by turning a very pleasing yellow. It could have many uses and will be mentioned later in various categories. 6 ft. by 3 ft. (2 m by 1 m). ZONES 6–8.

'Shaina' is a strange little tree, supposedly a sport of 'Bloodgood', but it does not look at all like it. It is small, twiggy and slow-growing, a good red color in both spring and fall. I do not have it in a container, but I think it would be well suited. 10 ft. by 6 ft. (3 m by 2 m). ZONES 6–8.

'Sherwood Flame' looks rather like its parent 'Burgundy Lace' but holds its spring color all season, rather than "greening." It has splendid fall foliage. 15 ft. by 15 ft. (5 m by 5 m). ZONES 6–8.

When I first saw 'Shin-deshojo' I could not believe that it was real. The spring color is a flaming, shouting scarlet that holds for quite a long time,

Top right: *Acer palmatum* 'Inazuma'
Bottom right: *Acer palmatum* 'Shaina'

Above: *Acer palmatum* 'Shin-deshojo'

then turns a sort of white and pink-speckled green, and in the fall a blend of red and orange. 6 ft. by 6 ft. (2 m by 2 m). ZONES 6–8.

'Sumi-nagashi' is a rich, dark purple in the spring, turning to deep maroon in the summer and gorgeous crimson red in the fall. Its dark early color makes a good contrast against other maples. 15 ft. by 12 ft. (5 m by 4 m). ZONES 6–8.

'Trompenburg' has leaves that are very different in shape, because they roll down, almost forming a tube. The color is a very rich purple-red, which lasts well into summer, then turns crimson. It is upright-growing and strong. 25 ft. by 15 ft. (8 m by 5 m). ZONES 6–8.

Red weeping maples
Perhaps for many people, what comes to mind at the mention of Japanese maples are weeping maples, those glorious, small, elegant trees that grace gardens, patios and containers the world over. These are **Acer palmatum var. dissectum,** and give

pleasure in inverse proportion to their size. They are budded onto a rootstock, which can be of varying heights to give a better cascading effect. It is not possible to give accurate heights and widths for these trees, because when you buy them they may have low or high rootstocks. However, as a general rule they will, in time, grow into a mushroom shape that will take many years to reach a width of 6 ft. (2 m). The branches will gradually mound up, increasing in height very slowly.

'Crimson Queen' is probably the most widely grown of all weeping maples, maybe because it holds its lovely red color all season, its intricate leaves are finely cut and its growth habit is very neat. In the fall it is bright scarlet. If you were so unfortunate as to be able to have just one maple, strong consideration would have to be given to 'Crimson Queen'. Even if you did not have much of a garden, it grows well in a container of a good size. In addition to all these virtues, it is strong-growing and comparatively hardy. However, this does not mean that you can grow it in a wind tunnel. ZONES 6–8.

There is some botanical discord about calling this maple **'Dissectum Atropurpureum'** because it covers more than one clone of several origins. However, what I purchased under this name is a most attractive and desirable plant, commonly known as the red lace leaf maple and probably the first red maple most of us knew. I particularly like it because it is not as densely branched as some maples, which makes it particularly graceful. It tends toward green during the summer. ZONES 6–8.

'Ever Red' (syn. 'Dissectum Nigrum') is rather similar to 'Crimson Queen', so you might ask, "Why grow it?" Well, because of the early spring growth, which is astonishingly beautiful. The new shoots are covered with silvery hairs, like no other maple, and therefore look gray. All too soon this changes to the usual dark red, and the tree is well named as its leaves remain red all season, crimson in the fall. ZONES 6–8.

I do not have a close acquaintance with the gemstone garnet but I understand that the weeping maple **'Garnet'** shares the rich red-purple with the gem and, what is more, holds its color well. I have noted with pleasure how vigorously it grows and how beautifully it cascades. ZONES 6–8.

I hope that I will not cause an uproar for suggesting that **'Red Dragon'** is indistinguishable from 'Crimson Queen', but perhaps it has a nicer name. In actual fact, the difference is that the leaves of 'Red Dragon' are a deeper color. ZONES 6–8.

'Red Filigree Lace' is just as pretty as it sounds, but unfortunately it is just so difficult to grow well. The experts praise it to the skies for it is so fine, so delicate, with its lacy leaves in dark red, which hold their color well. They admit, however, that it is slow-growing, and it is possible that I am not as good as I thought I was at growing maples. For whatever reason, where all other maples grow with

Top: *Acer palmatum* var. *dissectum* 'Garnet'
Above: *Acer palmatum* var. *dissectum* 'Red Dragon'

enthusiasm, dear little 'Red Filigree Lace' struggles. I am going to try it in a container, and perhaps this will solve my problems. ZONES 6–8.

It is probably stretching it a bit to call my next subject red, despite its name. **'Rubifolium'** is really green with red overtones. I am very fond of its subtlety, although the authors of *Maples of the World* do not care for it. ZONES 6–8.

The last red dissectum I am going to mention is called **'Tamukayama'**. It is a very old variety,

having been around since 1710. Its spring leaves are a beautiful crimson-red, soon turning to dark purple, then to a brilliant scarlet in the fall. The bark of the young branches is maroon, and the plant hardy and strong. ZONES 6–8.

These little weeping trees are quite special and have myriad uses, which we shall discuss in the chapter on landscaping.

The green selection

Green is a color that has a lot to offer even though the offering of green *Acer palmatum* is much smaller than that of the more blatant red. Having said this, there are some very choice green trees indeed. Green is such an important color, both in its own right and as a foil for brighter, showier subjects.

The first I will mention is the species itself, **Acer palmatum**, probably the green maple with which we are most familiar. It is an upright-growing tree with bright green foliage, and does not have any fussy hang-ups, except that, like all maples, it abhors wind. This description does not give you any idea of the grace and beauty the tree displays – the refined serrated leaves, the airy canopy and the brilliant fall colors.

There has been a perception that hybrids must be superior to species. This is very definitely not so – in fact, each case must be judged on its own merits. *Acer palmatum* really cannot be faulted, and it is wonderful to be able to grow the daddy of so many beautiful children.

The foliage on **'Hagaromo'** is dark green and is twisted in all directions and bushy in habit. To me it is a novelty I perhaps would not bother with until I had plenty of others. In fall its colors are pale yellow and orange. 12 ft. by 9 ft. (4 m by 2.7 m). ZONES 6–8.

A sort of cousin from South Korea is sometimes called **'Koreanum'** (or alternatively, 'Coreanum') and has the same excellent habits and bright fall color in orange, yellow and sometimes red. 25 ft. by 15 ft. (8 m by 5 m). ZONES 6–8.

Next is a very special tree that is certainly green in spring. **Acer palmatum** var. **heptalobum** is a sturdy, upright tree, which in the end, like many of us, spreads. But you should see the fall color – it is orange-scarlet, iridescent, luminous and wonderfully bright. 15 ft. by 20 ft. (5 m by 6 m). ZONES 6–8.

'Kamagata' grows in a very neat manner with green leaves that in the spring are margined in red. In the fall the colors are particularly pleasing in orange and yellow. 6 ft. by 3 ft. (2 m by 1 m). ZONES 6–8.

One of my favorite maples is **'Katsura'**. It is often listed as small or dwarf, but mine certainly are not. I think it must depend on climatic conditions, for Vertrees lists it as a dwarf, but *Maples of the World* remarks that in Europe it is not so. I just love it, from the moment in very early spring that it unfolds its beautiful orange-yellow leaves that are margined brighter orange, through summer green, on into the fall when it turns bright yellow and orange. A very similar cultivar is **'Orange Dream'**. 21 ft. by 10 ft. (7 m by 3 m). ZONES 6–8.

'Kotohime' is a sturdy, strong little plant that is particularly suited to rock gardens or containers. The leaves start orange-red, turn green and then a yellow gold. 3 ft. by 3 ft. (1 m by 1 m). ZONES 6–8.

'Koto-ito-komachi' is perhaps really for those of us who must have everything. It has threadlike skinny leaves, first red then green, followed by fall gold tones. It is not too readily available, being

Top: *Acer palmatum*
Above: *Acer palmatum* var. *heptalobum*

very difficult to propagate. If you could provide it with a nicely sheltered place it would certainly be a conversation piece. 3 ft. by 3 ft. (1 m by 1 m). ZONES 6–8.

Something different, because its bright green leaves are long and tapering, is **'Linearilobum'** (syn. 'Scolopendrifolium'). It is taller and slimmer than other maples – not so shrublike – with yellow fall foliage. It is a very pleasant tree. I have **'Linearilobum Rubrum'**, which has reddish leaves instead of

green – scarlet in the fall. I like it particularly because when the morning sun strikes it, it makes a nimbus of soft tan. I do not see this tree very often in other gardens so I am not sure that it is readily available. 15 ft. by 9 ft. (5 m by 2.7 m). ZONES 6–8.

'Lutescens' is a strong maple with very attractive bright green leaves in spring and glorious golden colors in the fall. 15 ft. by 10 ft. (5 m by 3 m). ZONES 6–8.

'Omurayama' is a bit of a puzzle. All the books say it cascades or weeps, but my two do not. It might be that either they have been grafted too low, or they should have been pruned up when young. A picture in J.D. Vertrees' splendid book shows a really beautiful, graceful tree that truly weeps. The new spring leaves – green with slight orange edges, then

Left: *Acer palmatum* 'Linearilobum'
Below: *Acer palmatum* 'Omurayama'

wholly green – are pretty. The fall color is gorgeous, a blend of yellow and scarlet. 21 ft. by 15 ft. (7 m by 5 m). ZONES 6–8.

'**Osakazuki**' is a tree with fall color that is supposed to be even better than *Acer palmatum* var. *heptalobum* – though this may be splitting leaves, so to speak. It is very famous, has been around since about 1850 and its fall color is something else. The leaves are green in spring and summer – quite pleasing without being over the top – but the fall color is an astounding intense crimson. I would be very unhappy without this treasure. 15 ft. by 15 ft. (5 m by 5 m). ZONES 6–8.

What I used to know as *Acer palmatum* '**Senkaki**' is now called '**Sango-kaku**', a name that means "coral tower." You grow it not so much for its pleasing green leaves, but for its stunning red-coral bark, which is at its most dramatic in the winter. I also love its fall color, for it is yellow, which makes a very pleasing contrast to all the more flamboyant oranges and reds. 25 ft. by 15 ft. (8 m by 5 m). ZONES 6–8.

Instead of being green, the leaves of '**Ukon**' are yellow-green, gradually turning to bright green. This maple is not very tall-growing, but is a pleasingly different color. The fall colors make such a good contrast with the reds because they are deep yellow and gold. 'Ukon' is not very common but deserves to be more widely grown. 9 ft. by 9 ft. (2.7 m by 2.7 m). ZONES 6–8.

In a way *Acer palmatum* '**Villa Taranto**' is neither fish nor fowl because, although it is basically green, it is, especially in the early spring, overlaid with the loveliest orange tan color. In summer it is green, in fall golden yellow. It has long, tapering leaves and would have to be described as exquisite. I would be bereft without it. 10 ft. by 5 ft. (3 m by 1.5 m). ZONES 6–8.

Acer palmatum 'Ukon'

Green weeping maples

It may be true to say that red maples are more attention grabbing than green, and perhaps at first glance this is understandable. However, a second look might show us that although green is a quieter color, more refined and subtle, it is also very beautiful. Aren't we fortunate that we do not have to choose but may have both?

The list of green weeping maples is not long but, like the upright type, it is very choice. As with other weeping maples, the rootstocks they are budded on to can be of varying heights so it is not possible to give accurate heights and widths for these trees. As a general rule they will grow into a mushroom shape, eventually reaching widths of 6–10 ft. (approximately 2–3 m) after many years. The height will very slowly increase as the branches mound up.

One of the most charming green weeping maples is '**Filigree**'. It is subtle and delicate in color, the leaf shade being green overlaid with flecks of gold or cream. The leaf itself is deeply dissected, which gives it its particularly lacy, fragile look. However, it is not fragile, it just gives the appearance of being so. I have four lining a woodland path and think they look delightful because they are on low standards,

suiting the path. If you were to feature 'Filigree' as a specimen it would be better to purchase a high grafted tree so its full cascading beauty could be seen and appreciated. The fall color is a rich yellow, which is more than acceptable since many maples are brighter, blessedly so certainly, but the contrast is beautiful, and so very useful in landscaping schemes. ZONES 6–8.

'**Flavescens**' is much sturdier-looking, the leaves more coarsely cut. These leaves are yellow-green in spring, turning darker in the summer and yellow tinged orange in the fall. Its cascading habit is particularly symmetrical. ZONES 6–8.

The weeping maple called '**Palmatifolium**' is a nice strong plant with rich green leaves. It is one of those plants that botanists debate about, some thinking it is really *dissectum* 'Paucem', others thinking it is just a strong selection of the species. Of more interest to the gardener is its impressive fall color of yellow, gold and crimson. ZONES 6–8.

There is but one upright *dissectum*. Unlike the other maples in this section, '**Seiryu**' does not actually weep. However, it looks very good planted among the weeping maples. It has bright green lacy foliage and its fall color is nothing short of a glory in gold, yellow and crimson. 9 ft. by 6 ft. (2.7 m by 2 m). ZONES 6–8.

In *Japanese Maples*, J.D. Vertrees wrote that the leaves of '**Sekimori**' are more feathery than lacy, which basically means they are coarser than most dissectums, but not as coarse as 'Palmatifolium' (though neither are really coarse, it is just a matter of degree). This is a good, sturdy little tree, which has fall leaves of a bright yellow-gold. ZONES 6–8.

Top left: *Acer palmatum* var. *dissectum* 'Viridis', or, as it is also known, *Acer palmatum* var. *dissectum*
Left: *Acer palmatum* var. *dissectum* 'Seiryu'

Above: *Acer palmatum* var. *dissectum* 'Filigree'
Right: *Acer palmatum* var. *dissectum* at the other end of the growing season

I did not know until recently that the species **Acer palmatum var. dissectum** and what I know as A. *p.* **'Viridis'** are actually one and the same thing. Gold colors adorn it in fall. ZONES 6–8.

Variegated maples

Variegated maples are very fancy indeed. How one's tastes can change – at one time I thought that variegated plants were a bit fussy, or even rather loud, not in astonishingly good taste. How wrong could I be? Many variegated plants are beautiful in their own right, with intricate markings in different colors, which prove their worth in many landscaping schemes, providing stunning contrast or brightening up dark (but not too dark) corners.

First is *Acer palmatum* **'Aka-shigitatsu-sawa'**, which is complex in its spring coloring. The leaves are deeply cut, wavy and sharply toothed, the color pinkish red with dark green veins. In fall it turns scarlet. 12 ft. by 6 ft. (4 m by 2 m). ZONES 6–8. The more usual form is **'Shigitatsu-sawa'**. More quietly colored in the spring with light green leaves and prominent-colored green veins, you would scarcely believe that it could turn blazing scarlet in the fall, but it does. 15 ft. by 9 ft. (5 m by 2.7 m). ZONES 6–8.

'Asahi-zuru' is not at all subtle. It has clearly defined, sharp variegation. The basic color is a good, strong green with white and pink markings. What intrigues me is that some leaves can be all white, some all green, many green with just flecks of pink and white, and in the spring some leaves are completely pink. 20 ft. by 9 ft. (6 m by 2.7 m). ZONES 6–8.

'Beni-schichihenge' is a little treasure, its name meaning "red and changeful." The leaves are green

Top: *Acer palmatum* 'Shigitatsu-sawa'
Above: *Acer palmatum* 'Asahi-zuru'

Right: *Acer palmatum* 'Beni-schichihenge'
Below right: *Acer palmatum* 'Higasayama'

with strong white margins, which does not sound so unusual, but what is startling is that the white is overprinted with a very distinct pinkish orange color. It is quite delicious, but not always readily available as it is, unfortunately, not easy to propagate. 10 ft. by 10 ft. (3 m by 3 m). ZONES 6–8.

'Butterfly' is a mixed-up kid, for her leaves are every which way. They are variable in shape and each lobe is different. The colors are green with cream edges, and in the fall the cream turns magenta, the green crimson. It is a most useful plant for small gardens, being dainty and pretty. I have used it to provide a little height in a small rock garden of cyclamen. 6–10 ft. by 5 ft. (2–3 m by 1.5 m). ZONES 6–8.

'Goshiki-kotohime' is variegated with green leaves speckled with cream, pink and red. It is red in fall, but you should only buy it if you are young because it grows at a snail's pace. 3 ft. by 3 ft. (1 m by 1 m). ZONES 6–8.

'Higasayama' has often been known by the name 'Roseomarginatum', which it is not. In fact, it does not even bear a passing resemblance to that variety. In early spring the cream leaves contrast strongly with their red sheaths – very different from any others and certainly very striking. Beautiful? I'm not quite sure, but it has its own attraction. The leaves develop an overlay of pink, then turn pale green and finish in fall in a blaze of orange and scarlet. Thus this tree has a lot to offer, especially for those who have a liking for something out of the ordinary. 15 ft. by 15 ft. (5 m by 5 m). ZONES 6–8.

'Kagero' is a highly regarded variegated maple, particularly because, instead of the usual white, its other color is yellow. The leaves are most variable, sometimes just a few yellow spots on the basic green

Top: *Acer palmatum* 'Peaches and Cream'

Above: *Acer palmatum* var. *dissectum* 'Ornatum Variegatum'

are bright green with cream markings. Its fall color is rather subdued in pale orange and red. 15 ft. by 10 ft. (5 m by 3 m). ZONES 6–8.

'Peaches and Cream' comes from Australia. It is small, and the foliage is pale green with touches of red and pink in the spring, turning dark green in summer, then orange and red in fall. It is not very easy to grow. 10 ft. by 10 ft. (3 m by 3 m). ZONES 6–8.

'Ukigumo' is not for everyone, for it is so heavily variegated in white and pink that I think the plant lacks chlorophyll and so, at least for me, it is a poor grower. However, it looks spectacular for a time in the spring. It is said by some authorities to be rising in popularity, so either it grows better in other climates, or I am not good at coping with it. 6 ft. by 6 ft. (2 m by 2 m). ZONES 6–8.

I grow only two variegated weeping maples but they are special – though I think one is more special than the other. *Acer palmatum* var. *dissectum* '**Ornatum Variegatum**' has a base color of green, overlaid with mostly white, sometimes showing a little pink. It is, as usual with weeping maples, very graceful, and because of its delicate coloring likes some protection from hot afternoon sun. ZONES 6–8.

But for me the really special variegated weeping maple is *Acer palmatum* var. *dissectum* '**Toyama-nishiki**'. It is not as commonly seen as 'Ornatum Variegatum' as it is very difficult to propagate. It has more intense colors, with a lot of pink as well as white on a greenish red base. It is delicately beautiful and it, too, would dislike hot afternoon sun. As with other weeping maples, their height is determined by the rootstock. ZONES 6–8.

leaf, or sometimes quite a solid amount of light yellow. There may also be all-yellow or all-green leaves – a really mixed-up plant! 10 ft. by 9 ft. (3 m by 2.7 m). ZONES 6–8.

'Orido-nishiki' in the early spring looks pink, and very fetching, too. Then other leaves appear that

Opposite: *Acer palmatum* var. *dissectum* 'Toyama-nishiki'

CHAPTER 3

Other Japanese Maples

A*cer palmatum* is not the only Japanese maple. I understand that although **Acer buergerianum** (trident maple) actually comes from China, it is always listed as Japanese. The ways of botanists are not always easy to follow, but the explanation of this anomaly is that Japanese horticulturists have developed a great many cultivars from the species, so you might say they have laid claim to it.

The species is very beautiful, classed as a small tree that does not mind dry conditions. As it copes with pollution well, it has been used most successfully as a streetside tree. It has shiny green leaves in spring (my particular one shows red coloration on the emerging leaves). The real glory of this tree, however, is in the fall when the colors turn to brilliant red and orange. If a tree has shiny leaves, as does this one, then the colors are more intense. 45 ft. by 25 ft. (14 m by 8 m). Zones 6–9.

Acer buergerianum has a number of named cultivars, most of which may not be readily available. There is a variegated form called **'Goshiki-kaede'**, which means "five-colored maple." The basic variegation is green with white. There is often pink in the new growth, which turns to cream or even yellow. It is semidwarf and stubby and would be excellent as a feature in a rock garden. 4^1/$_2$ ft. by 3 ft. (1.5 m by 1 m). Zones 6–9. There are a number of other cultivars, but they are generally not readily available.

Acer griseum

Acer griseum (paperbark maple), with its gorgeous peeling bark, is actually from China but is always listed in the nursery under Japanese maples, so that is how we will treat it. It is a loner without any varieties or cultivars and is grown mostly for its wonderful bark, hence its common name. The excoriating, or peeling, bark is dark orange-brown and, as it flakes off, the underbark shows its warm coppery color. Then the tree produces a stunning fall display of brilliant red, which lasts for a long time.

I often wondered why I did not see this splendid tree more often in gardens – I now know that it is very difficult to propagate, for it takes years for the seeds to germinate, and not much seed is actually

Opposite: *Acer rufinerve* 'Albolimbatum'

The fall colors of *Acer buergerianum*

viable. Growing from cuttings takes a great deal of skill, so *Acer griseum* is a treasure to be nurtured. 45 ft. by 9 ft. (14 m by 2.7 m). ZONES 4–8.

As has already been mentioned, there is a species called **Acer japonicum** (full-moon maple), which is noted particularly for its simply marvelous fall color. Strangely enough, there are not many varieties of *A. japonicum* available, but those that are easily found are absolutely stunning. The species itself is a small tree with smooth green leaves, purplish-red flowers and yellow-brown fruits, but the real glory is in the vibrant, rich crimson fall coloring. 30 ft. by 30 ft. (10 m by 10 m). ZONES 5–7.

My favorite *Acer japonicum* is **'Aconitifolium'**. It has leaves so deeply divided that they are described as "fernlike." The fern that it supposedly resembles would have to be of a sturdy type, but be that as it may, if you are going to grow but few maples this one would have to be given priority. The spring leaves are a deep green, and just before they appear the tree has the most gorgeous red flowers. However, the real glory is apparent in the fall when the leaves turn rich red and orange, a sight not easily forgotten. This tree does not grow fast. Still, it is quite undoubtedly one of the very choicest of maples, one that could hold its own with any tree you might mention. 36 ft. by 12 ft. (12 m by 4 m). ZONES 5–7.

There is a weeping form of *Acer japonicum* called **'Green Cascade'**, with deeply divided green leaves in spring and the astonishing colors of the japonicum in fall – red, yellow, crimson and orange. My plants grew very wide very suddenly so I was forced to move them. Give 'Green Cascade' plenty of space; if possible let it cascade down a bank and it will reward you handsomely by making an absolutely beautiful specimen. Height depends on the rootstock the cultivar is budded on to and width rarely exceeds 10 ft. (3 m) after many years. ZONES 6–8.

The only other *Acer japonicum* I grow is **'Vitifolium'**. "Vitis" is the botanical name for grape, and the leaves of *A. j.* 'Vitifolium' resemble those of grapevines. It is very sturdy and reputed to grow eventually to 23 ft. (7 m). The spring leaves are, as usual, green, but wait for the fall – the colors then are nothing short of magnificent, predominantly in gold with

Top: *Acer japonicum* 'Aconitifolium'
Above: *Acer japonicum* 'Green Cascade'

tones of scarlet and bright crimson. 23 ft. by 12 ft. (7 m by 4 m). ZONES 6–8.

Although I have mentioned but a few japonicums, they are so special that, if at all possible, grow every one. It would be an investment you would never regret.

Acer micranthum deserves to be grown in more gardens, but of course it is in a "Catch-22" situation. If there is no demand the tree will not be propagated, yet if gardeners do not ever see the subject they will not know about it and therefore won't want it. In these days of warehouses and supermarkets selling quick and easy plants at a discount, the whole horticultural trade has been skewed, and the future for superior, rare or special plants looks bleak.

However, should you be fortunate enough to find this treasure do not hesitate to buy it. It is a small deciduous tree with rusty red foliage in the early spring. The new stems and shoots are also rusty red, so it makes a most striking feature in any garden. Later on the leaves turn green and then, in fall, a stunning red. 20 ft. by 12 ft. (6 m by 4 m). ZONES 6–9.

Acer mono (syn. *A. cappadocicum* var. *mono*, *A. pictum*), the painted maple, is gorgeous but rather large, so is good for gardeners who would like a nice area of overhead shade for their borders. It has good, big leaves that are green until fall, whereupon they turn brilliant gold with crimson shading through them, giving rise to the epithet "painted."

There are many variations of *Acer mono*, depending upon which area of Japan is their natural habitat. However, it is very difficult to source them. If you can track down a specimen of *A. mono*, then buy it, not only for its outstanding fall beauty but also

Top left: The unusual green and white variegated leaves of *Acer rufinerve* 'Albolimbatum'
Left: *Acer shirasawanum* 'Autumn Moon'

to astonish your gardening friends. 40 ft. by 20 ft. (12 m by 6 m). ZONES 5–9.

Acer rufinerve (redvein maple) is a strong tree that is not too fussy as to where it grows. It has the most attractive green bark, which is striated (striped) white. The leaves are green, very acceptable, but the real glory comes in the fall when they turn yellow and gold with scarlet overtones – it is very striking indeed. 30 ft. by 30 ft. (10 m by 10 m). ZONES 6–9.

There are a few cultivars of *Acer rufinerve*, most of which are rare and just not available so they do not concern us. However, **'Albolimbatum'** is often seen and admired, for it is variegated in green and white in a rather irregular way. It does not grow quite as tall as the species, and its fall color is something else in purple and crimson. 30 ft. by 15 ft. (10 m by 5 m). ZONES 6–9.

From Australia comes a cultivar called **'Winter Gold'**. Its claim to fame is its lovely yellow bark, a color more intense in winter. The fall colors are yellow and dark orange. 25 ft. by 15 ft. (8 m by 5 m). ZONES 6–9.

Acer shirasawanum is a lovely tree. Its leaves are a light green, which make a good contrast to those that are darker. Then in the fall this small tree is ablaze in yellow and scarlet, fading to pale yellow in summer. The only word of warning I would sound is that this treasure will scorch in very hot sun, so it needs protection from the afternoon heat. 30 ft. by 20 ft. (10 m by 6 m). ZONES 5–8.

In contrast, the selected form **Acer shirasawanum 'Autumn Moon'** likes sun, which means that the light yellow leaves have rusty midribs. These are outstandingly attractive, the color most striking when the leaves are in sun. Those in the shaded parts of the plant will be yellow-green. The splendid fall leaves are the usual brilliant yellows and oranges. I think that if I were to choose just one of these lovely trees it would have to be A. s. 'Autumn Moon' because of its gorgeous color both in the spring and summer, its glorious fall color and the fact that it likes some sun. To have both the **'Full Moon'** and 'Autumn Moon' varieties would surely be bliss. 30 ft. by 20 ft. (10 m by 6 m). ZONES 5–8.

Acer sieboldianum is a stocky tree with foliage that is blue-green and covered in silky-looking hairs, which gives it its common name of silk canopy. In fall the leaves turn a brilliant orange and a luminous red. No serious collection of maples could do without this attractive subject, but as gardeners we are going to have to make some difficult choices because it seems to me that all Japanese maples are beautiful. In the end, just grow what you like best out of what is available; your choice will still be legion. 30 ft. by 20 ft. (10 m by 6 m). ZONES 3–8.

Acer tataricum subsp. **ginnala** (syn. *A. ginnala*), the Amur maple, is called a large shrub or small tree. It grows to about 30 ft. (10 m), and although this might seem to warrant the description of "tree" to many of us, this is not so. By definition a shrub is a many-branched plant, the branches coming from ground level, whereas a tree has a single stem with lateral branches. Be that as it may, *ginnala* would probably look like a sturdy tree to us. And sturdy it is for it happily copes with most situations. It has bright green leaves during spring and summer, then the most glorious brilliant orange and reds in the fall. 30 ft. by 25 ft. (10 m by 8 m). ZONES 3–7.

If you feel that you haven't space for this you need not despair for there is a dwarf *ginnala* called **'Durand Dwarf'**. It has been called a "burning bush" in the fall when its leaves turn the most arresting crimson. It would certainly be excellent in any garden, but is particularly suited to a small space or rock garden. 2 ft. by 1 ft. (60 cm by 30 cm). ZONES 3–7.

CHAPTER 4

Born in North America

North America has given us many beautiful deciduous trees and, of course, maples figure in this collection. Should you travel certain regions of North America in the fall you will be astonished at the blaze of orange, red and yellow in the forests. This kaleidoscope of brilliance is provided by a small tree (or rather, shrub) called **Acer circinatum** (vine maple), which looks rather like *A. japonicum*, but is stiffer in its habit of growth and its leaves are sticky. Also its flowers are colored wine and white, which is very striking. This small tree would be very acceptable in any garden. It is known as the vine maple because when it is overshadowed by large conifers in a forest it tends to wind its way up to the light, like a climbing vine. This would not happen in gardens, where it would be a large shrub with green leaves until the fall when its vibrant colors would be as beautiful as any of the Japanese treasures. 15 ft. by 20 ft. (5 m by 6 m). ZONES 6–9.

'Little Gem', which is a dwarf form of the species, will delight those with small gardens, rock gardens or both. It has all the attributes of *Acer circinatum*, it's just smaller and very slow-growing, rounded and bushy. I think this little tree would be splendid in a tub, or perhaps twin tubs at a front entrance, making an innovative change from the usual plants that grace such places. 3 ft. by 2 ft. (100 cm by 60 cm). ZONES 6–9.

'Monroe' is different again, for it is dissected, with deeply cut leaves rather like *Acer japonicum*

Opposite: *Acer rubrum* 'Armstrong II'

In the background at left, the rich colors of *Acer negundo* 'Flamingo'

'Aconitifolium'. It was not discovered until 1960, in the Cascade Mountains on North America's west coast, the only one of its kind ever found. I am not sure how readily available it is, and I have only seen photos of it, but it sounds special. It will grow into a tall bush. 12 ft. by 9 ft. (4 m by 2.7 m). ZONES 6–9.

Acer glabrum is not widely grown, which is a pity, for it is a very attractive large shrub. The subspecies, **A. g. douglasii**, is even more attractive because the young shoots are bright red, whereas in the species they are purple. The fall leaves are a clear yellow, which would make a wonderful psychedelic picture teamed with all the reds, russets and oranges of so many of the other maples. 20 ft. by 12 ft. (6 m by 4 m). ZONES 5–8.

Acer negundo (ash-leaved maple, box elder, Manitoba maple) comes from North America where

it is naturalized, as it also is in China and South America. I am not going to suggest this large tree for your garden but rather tell you about some very good varieties that are readily available. 50 ft. by 30 ft. (15 m by 10 m). ZONES 5–8.

'Elegans' is a small tree whose green leaves have creamy margins. It has an elegant poise and a quiet grace. 23 ft. by 12 ft. (7 m by 4 m). ZONES 5–8.

Rather more flamboyant is 'Flamingo'. The leaves of this splendid selection are green with lots of pink when they are young. They then tend to have cream margins with hints of pink. In fall, red and pink are the most desirable colors. All in all, this tree looks graceful because of its coloring, and given a dark background it is quite spectacular. It will also add great interest to a dull part of the garden. I highly value the two I grow. 20 ft. by 12 ft. (6 m by 4 m). ZONES 5–8.

'Kelly's Gold', which hails from Duncan & Davies of New Plymouth, New Zealand, is lovely, for its color is a soft yellow in spring, then lime green and

Above: An avenue of *Acer rubrum*
Above right: The flower tassels of *Acer negundo* 'Violaceum'

finally buttery yellow in the fall. It is another pretty tree with color that will contrast so satisfactorily with the darker green or reds of so many others. 5 ft. by 9 ft. (1.5 m by 2.7 m). ZONE 5.

'Violaceum' is quite startling in the spring for it has long racemes of reddish pink flower tassels. You could well grow it for this reason alone, but this generous tree also produces violet-colored

new shoots covered in a white bloom – the leaves then turn green in spring, gold in fall. 40 ft. by 27 ft. (12 m by 9 m). ZONE 5.

There are many other varieties of *Acer negundo*, most so rare (and maybe not so special) that they are not in cultivation, but those mentioned, should you decide to grow them, will give you both interest and pleasure.

Acer pensylvanicum (moosewood, striped maple), as you would guess, comes from eastern North

America, and is the only "snakebark" maple that does not come from Asia. Its bark is truly astonishing. The green bark is marked with wide white stripes and is even more striking in winter when the bark turns reddish brown, the white stripes very distinct. It is a bonus to have a deciduous tree with such winter interest and, what is more, the winter buds are red. Add to this that A. *pensylvanicum* has very large leaves that turn a lovely yellow in the fall and you can certainly see why it has become very popular, particularly in the United States. 25 ft. by 18 ft. (8 m by 6 m). ZONES 4–6.

There is a gorgeous cultivar of *Acer pensylvanicum* called **'Erythrocladum'**, which has the most wonderful salmon-red to crimson twigs in winter, but unfortunately is very difficult to propagate, so it would be a lucky person who managed to source and buy it. Both A. *pensylvanicum* and cultivar 'Erythrocladum' loathe lime soil. 18 ft. by 12 ft. (6 m by 4 m). ZONES 6–8.

Acer rubrum (red maple, scarlet maple) is a glorious tree, but it is very large. It grows naturally all through eastern North America and, as its name suggests, it is brilliant red in the fall. Many varieties have colors ranging through red, orange and yellow, a quite unbelievable sight in autumn.

It is surely evident that this tree is not for the small garden, but your garden would not have to be huge to accommodate just one, especially as some varieties are columnar. Other than the marvelous fall display, the tree has gorgeous red flowers in spring. As these are displayed on naked branches, the sight is arresting. Height 70 ft. by 30 ft. (20 m by 10 m). ZONES 4–9.

Because *Acer rubrum* is so popular in its home country, many superior selections have been made, giving us gardeners a wide choice. One variety is **'Armstrong'**, which grows into a narrow column, thus being a good choice where there is limited space.

Acer rubrum 'October Glory'

An even narrower version is called **'Armstrong II'**. 70 ft. by 12 ft. (20 m by 4 m). ZONES 4–9.

'Bowhall' is also columnar in habit, growing to only about 50 ft. (15 m), so it is a useful size without being too overwhelming. Its fall coloring is the usual astonishing blaze. 50 ft. by 12 ft. (15 m by 4 m). ZONES 4–9.

Perhaps the best *Acer rubrum* is **'October Glory'**, whose brilliant red fall color is intense and lasts longer on the tree than some of the others. It grows too fast for its own good, making it a bit soft, so needs some protection from wind. Where I have planted 'October Glory' in poor soil it is slower growing, so does not have a problem with breaking branches, which can be distressing where the tree grows fast. But I have to say that I would rather some branches of 'October Glory' break than not have the tree at all. I would be bereft without it. 50 ft. by 20 ft. (15 m by 6 m). ZONES 4–9.

'Red Sunset' is considered quite outstanding, with larger leaves than usual and a broad pyramidal crown. As you would expect, the fall color is an intense red. 70 ft. by 30 ft. (20 m by 10 m). ZONES 3–9.

'Scanlon' is upright, very well-known, widely grown and stunning in the fall in orange, crimson and purple. 50 ft. by 15 ft. (15 m by 5 m). Zones 4–9.

'Schlesingeri' – such a name – is an old cultivar (1886), which has stood the test of time because of its splendid fall color in orange, yellow and lovely dark wine red. 70 ft. by 30 ft. (20 m by 10 m). Zones 4–9.

These mentioned are the varieties I know best, but many more selected varieties are also available. However, I cannot imagine that they could be any more beautiful.

A wonderful tree in this same style is a hybrid between *Acer rubrum* and *A. saccharinum*. Known as **Acer x freemanii**, it was so named after Oliver Freeman, a plant breeder from the U.S. National Arboretum who made this stunning cross, although later it was found occurring naturally where the parent species were growing. 50 ft. by 30 ft. (15 m by 10 m). Zones 5–8.

'Autumn Blaze' is upright and narrow, growing rather fast, with orange leaves in the fall, a most wonderful color. 50 ft. by 25 ft. (15 m by 8 m). Zones 5–8.

'Autumn Fantasy' has brilliant flowers in spring, as well as stunning fall colors. 50 ft. by 30 ft. (15 m by 10 m). Zones 5–8.

'Marmo' also has attractive spring flowers, and orange and yellow coloration in the fall. 50 ft. by 25 ft. (15 m by 8 m). Zones 5–8.

Above right: The large, intensely colored leaves of *Acer rubrum* 'Red Sunset'
Right: The fallen leaves of *Acer rubrum* 'Scanlon'

So it can be seen that if you wish to grow *Acer rubrum* or its hybrids you have a wide and exciting choice. I have had a great deal of pleasure out of my small collection.

Acer saccharinum (syn. *A. dasycarpum*), the silver maple or soft maple, hails from eastern North America. It is a graceful tree with green leaves, which are glaucous underneath, and lovely light gray fissured bark (where the term "silver" must come from – as well as the fact that when the wind blows you can see the silvery undersides of the leaves). 80 ft. by 50 ft. (25 m by 15 m). ZONES 4–9.

However, *Acer saccharinum* is rather brittle and inclined to break in the wind. Also, it has a nasty reputation for doing unspeakable damage to drains and paving. So why mention it? Because there are some very desirable cultivars, one of which is **'Born's Gracious'**, certainly a lovely name that you would not be inclined to forget. This tree is a little pendulous, which makes it most graceful. It has yellow fall color. If I could grow just one silver maple, for me 'Born's Gracious' would be it. 60 ft. by 20 ft. (18 m by 6 m). ZONES 4–9.

Acer saccharinum 'Lutescens' has yellow leaves in spring, turning green and then golden yellow in the fall. 50 ft. by 30 ft. (15 m by 10 m). ZONES 4–9.

Acer saccharum (hard maple, rock maple, sugar maple) is a lovely tree and you need not be passionate about maple syrup to grow it. This quite large tree is considered to be one of North America's finest deciduous trees for fall color in shades of crimson, gold, orange and scarlet. Do not despair about size for there are some stunning varieties that do not grow too tall for most gardens. 70 ft. by 40 ft. (20 m by 12 m). ZONES 4–8.

'Bonfire' grows faster than most of its kind. Its fall colors – red, orange and orange-red – explain its name. 46 ft. by 21 ft. (14 m by 7 m). ZONES 4–8.

Acer x freemanii 'Autumn Blaze'

'Brocade' makes a striking contrast. It is a smaller grower, sporting golden-yellow fall leaves. 30 ft. by 15 ft. (10 m by 5 m). ZONES 4–8.

I have not seen **'Newton Sentry'** (syn. 'Columnaire') but I liked the description in *The Hillier Manual of Trees and Shrubs*, which said that it was a pillar of orange in the early fall. This sounded most delectable to me. Other than that it is slow-growing, has no central leader and is very narrow. 30 ft. by 8 ft. (10 m by 2.5 m). ZONES 4–8.

There are other maples that call North America home, such as **Acer macrophyllum** (big-leaf maple, Oregon maple) and **A. spicatum** (mountain maple), but these are not suitable garden subjects nor are they readily available. This should not be of concern as the maples that have been described are so beautiful that we should not want for more.

CHAPTER 5

Maples from Other Lands

Not all garden-worthy maples come from either Japan or North America, so I will discuss some beautiful subjects from other lands.

Acer acuminatum comes from the Himalayas, a source of so many of the beautiful plants grown today, particularly magnolias. It is a small deciduous tree that has bright green leaves, yellowish green flowers and the usual winged seeds. It has good fall color and therefore would be a pleasant addition to a maple collection. 40 ft. by 20 ft. (12 m by 6 m). ZONES 5–7.

Acer campestre is known as the hedge maple and was used to form hedges in Britain. It has the usual desirable attributes of maples in leaves, flowers and seeds, and yellow, sometimes tinged red, fall color. I do not know if people in Britain clipped their hedges, but if you lived in the country and could leave them untouched they would be quite spectacular. There are differently colored versions of *A. campestre*: **'Carnival'** (variegated green leaves, edged pink and white) 9 ft. by 9 ft. (2.7 by 2.7 m); **'Postelense'** (yellow leaves, red stalks) 9 ft. by 6 ft. (2.7 m by 2 m); **'Pulverulentum'** (leaves blotched and speckled white) 12 ft. by 9 ft. (4 m by 2.7 m). ALL ZONES 5–8.

Acer cappadocicum (Cappadocian maple, Caucasian maple, coliseum maple) is too large for most gardens, as it grows up to 70 ft. (20 m) high, but *A. c.* **'Aureum'**, although eventually growing tall, is quite different. It is slow-growing, comes from

Acer pseudoplatanus 'Esk Sunset'

Central Europe and rejoices in the most astonishing spring leaves in coppery red, turning yellow, then green, and in fall, yellow-red. You could scarcely ask for more. 50 ft. by 30 ft. (15 m by 10 m). ZONES 5–8.

The variety called **'Rubrum'** has blood-red spring leaves, turning green, then red in fall. What a wonderful pair these two would make. 50 ft. by 30 ft. (15 m by 10 m). ZONES 5–8.

Acer x conspicuum (*A. davidii* x *A. pensylvanicum*) would have to be beautiful because it was bred by two world authorities: van Gelderen and Oterdoom. It is a small tree, its real claim to fame being its stunning striped bark. There are several named cultivars: **'Elephant's Ear'** has purple bark with

49

Above: *Acer platanoides* 'Crimson King'
Left and below left: The spring and fall leaf colors of
Acer davidii

white stripes; **'Phoenix'** has striped bark and bright red new stems; and **'Silver Vein'** has bluish green bark, striped white. Striped bark is particularly valuable and beautiful in winter when there is less to see in the garden and you can really examine the intricacy of the patterns. 26 ft. by 20 ft. (8 m by 6 m). ZONES 6–8.

Acer davidii (Père David's maple) is one of my favorite trees, and it also has striped bark – green and white. It has a spreading habit and has quite large, more or less heart-shaped leaves, which are a coppery green when they first unfold, then a rich, deep green. The flowers hang in long racemes in a most attractive manner and the fall colors are striking in yellow, red and purple. This tree has real elegance and I plan to never be without it. 50 ft. by 50 ft. (15 m by 15 m). ZONES 5–7.

Acer morrisonensis is yet another snakebark, or striped-bark tree, this one hailing from Taiwan. The leaves open red, turn green, then turn orange and red in fall. The stems are bright red, so it is not difficult to see how desirable this small tree is and how well it would fit into a group of specially selected maples. 20 ft. by 12 ft. (6 m by 4 m). ZONES 6–8.

Acer platanoides is known as the Norway maple and it is huge, and so is not for average-sized gardens. Luckily there are many cultivars that can fit into larger gardens. 80 ft. (25 m) by 50 ft. (25 m by 15 m). ZONES 3–7.

The flower of *Acer platanoides* (above) and the beautiful fall leaf color (below).

Probably the best-known and most popular cultivar of *Acer platanoides* is **'Crimson King'**, which has red-purple leaves and brilliant scarlet fall color, supposedly the best of all red-leafed Norway maples. It grows to a reasonably modest height after about 20 years. As a bonus, it has very pretty flowers, yellow with a tinge of red. 40 ft. by 25 ft. (12 m by 8 m). ZONES 3–7.

A cultivar of 'Crimson King' is called **'Crimson Sentry'** probably because it is fastigiate (upright). Although I have not seen it, it is said to be smaller-growing so would be grand in smaller gardens. 40 ft. by 15 ft. (12 m by 5 m). ZONES 3–7.

There are actually a great number of named cultivars of *Acer platanoides* but I will mention just one more. **'Drummondii'** (harlequin maple) would suit either large or small gardens. It has green and white variegated leaves, making it beautiful in its own right, and so useful as a contrast or foil. 30–40 ft. by 30–40 ft. (10–12 m by 10–12 m). ZONES 3–7.

Acer pseudoplatanus (planetree maple, syca-more maple) is the sycamore. Before you start shuddering with horror, let me assure you that I would not dream of recommending you grow this giant, but there are some gorgeous cultivars that

grow to a more reasonable size. 100 ft. by 80 ft. (30 m by 25 m). ZONES 4–7.

'Brilliantissimum' is well named, for in the spring the new leaves unfold shrimp-pink, turn yellow-green and finally green. It is gorgeous but a bit fussy – it does not like too much hot sun, which causes it to burn, so it needs protection. It is well worth a little extra trouble. It is a tree of leisure, for it is very slow-growing. 20 ft. by 25 ft. (6 m by 8 m). ZONES 4–7.

From New Zealand comes a very beautiful variety called **'Esk Sunset'**. The leaves are strongly mottled pink in the spring, and as the season progresses the undersides turn the most fetching burgundy. It is very slow-growing and deserves to be planted in a prominent place for it never fails to attract attention. 15 ft. by 10 ft. (5 m by 3 m). ZONES 5–8.

From the same stable comes **'Esk Flamingo'**, also mottled, but in green and white, its outstanding feature being its gorgeous red twigs. 15 ft. by 10 ft. (5 m by 3 m). ZONES 5–8.

'Leopoldii' grows larger than 'Brilliantissimum'. Its leaves are mottled and splashed white and yellow, showing pinkish tinges in early spring. 25 ft. by 18 ft. (8 m by 6 m). ZONES 4–7.

A close relative of 'Brilliantissimum' is **'Prince Handjery'**, which is similar but its leaves are tinted purple underneath. 15 ft. by 6 ft. (5 m by 2 m). ZONES 4–7.

There are hundreds of maples I have not mentioned that are actually not suited for home gardens. However, those described provide riches enough from which to choose.

Top: *Acer pseudoplatanus* 'Brilliantissimum'
Above: *Acer pseudoplatanus* 'Esk Flamingo'

Opposite: *Acer pseudoplatanus* 'Esk Sunset'

CHAPTER 6

Landscaping with Maples

The large garden

Small and large gardens require very different treatments, so we shall have fun landscaping a mythical large garden first. What is large? Probably anything over an acre (approximately 4,000 sq m). Let us pretend that we have an empty yard with just a house, paths and fences. This yard just happens to be on a slope. Certainly, it also needs shelter from vicious winds, so let's imagine that the yard has hedges and shelter trees. Not everyone likes the same tree to the same degree, so I will first suggest what I would like and have found to be successful in my garden.

Acer palmatum

I truly think that there is no more beautiful tree to grace gardens – either small or large – than the Japanese maple. It would be splendid to plant in groups of several of each variety, but not many people have that amount of land available for just one type of tree, so I would suggest a mixed planting.

I would make a grove of about 15 trees and mix them for color and variety. To choose just one maple would be very difficult indeed, but a group allows for a lot less difficulty in decision-making.

First I would choose *Acer palmatum* 'Shindeshojo' (page 23) because of its wonderful variation in color, particularly throughout the spring. I would have three of this beauty, although I would obviously have to reject two other trees to do this.

Opposite: A lovely combination of mostly *Acer palmatum* varieties planted along a grassed walkway

Maples and water always work well together.

Nor would I plant them in a group, which is, of course, sound landscaping idiom. Instead, I would place them individually among the others.

Acer palmatum are, of course, small trees, and what I would plant vary between about 10–15 ft. (3–5 m) in height, so it is not critical as to where to plant the selection. I recommend planting them about 15 ft. (5 m) apart, which will mean that it will still be easy to mow the grass and that the full beauty of each tree may be appreciated. I feel strongly about this – and here experience is speaking – because my grove is too close together. This means that there will be some agonizing decisions later as to what to take out, and also the grass tends to get overshaded. This probably does not matter too much, but a pleasant green sward sets the planting off.

Above: The bright red color of *Acer palmatum* 'Beni-otake'
Left: *Acer palmatum* 'Shin-deshojo'

listed in the table on page 57 (full descriptions are given in earlier chapters).

Trees can be planted, as mentioned, amidst grass, but of course the planting could be in a cultivated border, the maples providing the height and scope for companion planting (see Chapter 7).

North American maples

Any North American species or cultivars chosen for the small- to average-sized garden could also grace the larger garden, but there are some beautiful trees that require a good deal of space. This might be a big garden that needs some statuesque trees, or you might have some acres or even a whole farm to play with.

If so, I would immediately plant the glorious *Acer rubrum*. Even in a big garden, I would probably have to choose just one, so I would settle for a variety

When choosing which varieties to plant, I have considered both spring and fall colors, plain and variegated, all to be randomized. As already mentioned, because of its amazing changes of color I will plant three 'Shin-deshojo', scattered through the planting, noting that its fall color is a gorgeous red. The other selections, arbitrarily chosen by me (you may like different varieties altogether) are

Acer palmatum cultivars

Cultivar	Height	Colors
A. p. 'Beni-otake'	10 ft. (3 m)	red in spring and fall
A. p. 'Bloodgood'	15 ft. (5 m)	red, then scarlet
A. p. 'Higasayama'	15 ft. (5 m)	variegated, then orange and scarlet
A. p. var. *heptalobum*	15 ft. (5 m)	green, then scarlet
A. p. 'Kagero'	10 ft. (3 m)	variegated, then gold
A. p. 'Katsura'	21 ft. (7 m)	yellow, orange, then gold and orange
A. p. 'Lutescens'	15 ft. (5 m)	yellow-green, then rich yellow
A. p. 'Okagami'	12 ft. (4 m)	red, then scarlet
A. p. 'Osakazuki'	15 ft. (5 m)	green, then brilliant scarlet
A. p. 'Seiryu'	9 ft. (2.7 m)	green, then gold and crimson
A. p. 'Shigitatsu-sawa'	15 ft. (5 m)	variegated, then scarlet
A. p. 'Villa Taranto'	10 ft. (3 m)	green then gold

called 'Bowhall' because it is very upright and the fall colors are out of this world.

Then I would attend to the rest of the property and plant groups that would certainly look good all year, but in the fall would be unbelievable. I would have three each of 'October Glory' and 'Armstrong II'. Then, perhaps two of the outstanding 'Red Sunset' followed by two 'Scanlon' and three 'Schlesingeri'. As companions I would have the hybrid *Acer* x *freemanii*, three 'Autumn Blaze' and a couple of 'Autumn Fantasy'. What a sight they would be.

You might feel that your garden could do with more than one of these maples. Rest assured that any of them would look superb.

I do not think I would plant the species *Acer saccharinum* but rather concentrate on some grand cultivars – two specifically that would represent the so-called silver maples. The first one is 'Born's Gracious', a tree that grows prettily in a pendulous manner with golden fall color. The other is 'Lutescens', with yellow leaves.

Acer saccharum, the sugar maple, is considered one of North America's finest trees for fall color

Right: *Acer rubrum* 'Scanlon'

so I would grow it but, because it is very large, only out in the farm paddock. Then in the garden there could also be 'Bonfire', 'Brocade' and 'Newton Sentry' because they have such color – red, orange or yellow. In North America there are many more varieties of *A. saccharum* but I think these three are quite outstanding and would do a North American garden very proud indeed.

The small garden

For those with small gardens, carefully choosing trees is very important, because you do not have the space for mistakes. However, I do not think that you can have a proper garden without some trees, otherwise it will be lacking in height and charisma. Because space is limited, instead of choosing just one or two comparatively large trees, it is certainly possible to have perhaps half a dozen small, choice specimens.

Acer palmatum

In comparative terms, *Acer palmatum* are small trees, but some are so small as to be more like shrubs. These have their place in gardens, obviously being well-suited to the modern little patch. These plants have a multitude of uses, as in the rock garden, in containers, for bonsai and in the perennial border. Should you have a small water feature these dainty trees could well make your pond special.

There are the small upright *Acer palmatum*, as well as the weeping maples *A. p.* var. *dissectum* that you might think were specially designed for restricted spaces. These trees would best not stand alone, but would be incorporated in a mixed border – at least the upright growers. The weeping trees could be used a little differently if you wished.

'Aratama' grows to only about 3 ft. (1 m) with spring leaves of a most stunning red. Next I would highly recommend 'Beni-komachi', which is the

Above right: *Acer palmatum* 'Beni-hime'
Right: *Acer palmatum* 'Aratama'

Acer palmatum 'Beni-komachi'

most brilliant red in both spring and fall. The next trees I will mention share the same coloring and would be very difficult to resist when choosing for the small garden. At 3 ft. (1 m), 'Beni-hime' is little but not delicate, and the red is pink-red to a sort of rusty color. 'Beni-maiko' is the most arresting scarlet pink in spring, scarlet in fall. The only catch is that this absolute treasure may be very difficult to source. 'Beni-schichihenge' is variegated in a most entrancing manner, its green leaves overlaid with pinkish orange and its margins white. 'Chishio' is smaller at about 10 ft. (3 m) and also rejoices in brilliant red early coloring, then orange-scarlet in fall. The last red I shall mention is called 'Pixie' and

is new to me. It looks like a little 'Bloodgood', which is a real recommendation.

After all these reds for the small garden I think it is time to mention some small-growing greens. 'Kamagata' is deservedly popular, with light green leaves in summer, but in the spring the edges of the leaves are a rusty red. In fall its dress is yellow and orange – very pleasant indeed.

'Ukon' does not grow very tall, only about 9 ft. (2.7 m), and it is a very pleasant yellow-green color, different from the more usual green. In the fall it displays colors of deep gold with red tones in some leaves. It would make a lovely contrast with the varieties already mentioned.

Acer palmatum var. *dissectum*

Acer rubrum

The weeping maples are delightful subjects for any garden, but perhaps never more so than in a small garden. This is a good, readily available selection in green, reds and variegated so it is just a matter of choosing. Descriptions of these can be found in Chapter 2.

North American maples
If we create a garden with lawns and borders that are fortuitously empty of trees and make a small- to average-sized portion of it what in modern jargon is called "themed," we could have a part devoted to North America.

Start with *Acer circinatum*, the vine maple, because it is a shrub with astonishing fall color. If you think a height of 15 ft. (5 m) is not what you want, go for 'Little Gem', which, at only 3 ft. (1 m), would be absolutely ideal for the front of a border, and yet still rejoices in all the good attributes of the species.

The species *Acer negundo* is too large for this particular garden but there are some lovely varieties that would lend real charisma to our planting. First of all, plant a couple of variegated trees, so useful for contrast and for lightening up a dull corner. *A. negundo* 'Elegans' and 'Flamingo', the first green

and cream, the second green and pink with cream and lovely fall hues of red and pink, are generous trees. 'Kelly's Gold' is gold, or rather a soft yellow, providing some lovely less usual colors in the North American corner. The last *A. negundo* I would plant, *A. n.* 'Violaceum', has long racemes of reddish pink flowers or tassels, which are very striking, and good fall color, this time gold.

To carry on the North American theme with unusual characteristics I would plant *Acer pensylvanicum* because it has such wonderful snakebark, striped in green and white, which looks particularly sharp in winter. All my choices have unusual features so I think this North American-themed section will look very fine.

Landscaping with *Acer japonicum*
There are a great number of garden subjects that look their very best in the spring, but not quite so many that show their full glory in the fall. One such is *Acer japonicum* and its cultivars, which, although beautiful in spring and summer, are absolutely stunning in their fall glory.

In Chapter 3 I described those I know that are readily available, and I suggest, if at all possible, that you grow the lot. I will discuss three varieties only, so set aside a little corner of the garden and group them together – it will look lovely.

As *Acer japonicum* will grow to about 30 ft. (10 m), I would place a couple as background, where they would flame in the fall in gold with a touch of crimson. Then I would have three 'Aconitifolium', surely one of the most beautiful maples. The deeply cut leaves are beautiful at any time but never more so than in fall when the colors are a scintillating, reverberating red and orange.

To finish off the special grouping I would turn to the weeping form 'Green Cascade'. As this plant

Clockwise from top right: *Acer japonicum* 'Aconitifolium'; *Acer japonicum* 'Green Cascade'; *Acer japonicum* 'Aconitifolium'; *Acer japonicum* 'Green Cascade'.

Acer palmatum 'Bloodgood'

spreads very amply I think that just one would suffice. It would also provide colors of red, yellow, crimson and orange so that the patch would always look beautiful, but in the fall would blaze with glory. It would be just the time to ask friends to an al fresco meal to share the beauty of *Acer japonicum*.

Landscaping with maples from other lands

Although I would like to pretend that my maple garden has unlimited space, I know that this is not the case. The ideas I put before you are for your consideration and if you like them you can pick and choose to suit yourself. This allows me to mention rather more than most gardeners would be able to grow.

First in this category of acers that do not come from either Japan or North America, I think the two *Acer cappadocicum* mentioned in Chapter 5, 'Aureum' and 'Rubrum', should be planted together for striking contrast.

Then there are the snakebarks, all lovely, but which to choose? Well, I certainly could not be without *Acer davidii*, and in a little group we could have two others. Let's settle for *Acer* x *conspicuum* 'Phoenix' and the strangely named 'Elephant's Ear'. This grouping will look quite special at all times of the year with great interest in the winter when the beautiful bark may be closely observed.

In *Acer platanoides* I would want to grow the brilliant 'Crimson King' and perhaps find a space for 'Drummondii' because its green and white leaves would go well most anywhere.

In what would surely be called the ornamental *Acer pseudoplatanus*, I would have a glorious grouping made up of 'Esk Sunset', with 'Brilliantissimum' given the shadiest space, and 'Esk Flamingo' rounding out the trio. Mottled, spotted pink, green, white and burgundy – what a glorious sight. Before I get too enthusiastic I do have to mention that you can more or less forget fall color with this grouping, but it is easy to forgive them for they are so generous over the rest of the year.

Maples and water

Bodies of water and graceful maples complement each other so beautifully. Water features can range from a large lake to tiny ponds, with graduations in between. Not many of us have a large lake but many people do have a pond, with perhaps a fountain or a little stream. All these can be greatly enhanced by maples as perimeter plantings.

For large-scale water features, upright maples look splendid – in addition to their beauty of leaf and form you may have the joy of reflections on the water. If you have considerable space you can afford to plant your maples a good distance apart, allowing the trees to display their full glory.

For the smaller water feature the same premise applies – less is more. If you have just a little pond, perhaps not much more than a big sunken container,

a weeping maple would transform something quite ordinary into a delightful addition to the garden. If you happen to be so very fortunate as to have a waterfall, a weeping maple gracefully leaning over makes a charming picture.

It is interesting to note that most books that I have read about water gardening concentrate on marginal plants suited to growing in or around water, and do not mention trees. It seems to me that the addition of suitable trees lifts the whole concept to a higher plane. There is no more suitable tree than *Acer palmatum* to achieve this.

A beautiful planting of *Acer palmatum* var. *dissectum* by a bend in the stream

CHAPTER 7

Companion Planting

Many plants make suitable companions for maples. The root system of maples is fibrous and not too deep, so companion plants will not have aggressive competition from these trees. Also their roots are not right near the surface so there is no problem planting companions underneath. I will start with some choice trees, then discuss shrubs, perennials and bulbs, because unless you are an absolute maple fanatic, monoculture is not a good idea.

Trees planted by themselves, amidst a mowed lawn, do not make a garden. Such a planting is better described as a park, or, if not very large, what could be called "park-like." This book refers acers in garden settings. So, what turns a park into a garden? My dictionary defines a garden as a "piece of ground adjoining a house, typically cultivated to provide a lawn and flower beds." Even this definition I consider too limiting, as many gardens have little or no lawn, and in my opinion no cultivated space is worthy of the name garden if it does not incorporate trees – even if it is just one in a container in a small courtyard or balcony.

Trees

I will not mention too many trees because I have some beautiful and unusual shrubs waiting in the wings. As previously mentioned, you cannot and will not want to grow everything I suggest. I just hope what I include will give you some inspiration.

Opposite: *Acer rubrum* 'October Glory' at left, with *Cercis canadensis* 'Forest Pansy' at right

The wonderful fall colors of *Cercis canadensis* 'Forest Pansy' complement those of maples extremely well.

In these few but very important trees I cannot fail to mention a North American tree that I think rivals any acer for beauty – **Cercis canadensis** (eastern redbud). The variety **'Forest Pansy'** has very large heart-shaped leaves in the most delectable wine-red. In the fall, surprisingly, these stunning leaves turn orange and yellow. In gardening terms I think it one of the wonders of the world and I hope never to garden without it.

Both the North American **Cornus florida** (flowering dogwood) and the Japanese **C. kousa** (Kousa dogwood) complement maples, particularly the Japanese acers, beautifully. C. *florida* flowers on bare branches when the maples are in early leaf. The "flowers" are really wide, flat bracts in white, pink

65

Nyssa sylvatica 'Sheffield Park'

or red, quite beautiful; then fall brings a spectacular display of color. *C. kousa* flowers a little later, which is excellent, and its smaller leaves turn a glowing red in fall.

I think any or all *Cornus* varieties are gorgeous, but if forced to choose a few I would settle for the following. The hybrid **'Eddie's White Wonder'** for its white flowers surrounded by white bracts, and the tree's semi-weeping or pendulous form – it goes without saying that its fall color is bright and beautiful. **'Cherokee Chief'** has nearly red flowers, and wonderful fall color of yellow, scarlet and wine-red. If I were limited to three *C. florida* I would have to include the variegated **'Cherokee Sunset'** because the yellow and green variegations turn such unbelievable colors in the fall – reds and oranges. I have to say that it has been very slow to flower but I think the pretty leaves make up for that.

In my choice of *Cornus kousa* there is no soul searching. **'Satomi'** has huge pink bracts that are truly gorgeous, and then good fall color. Of course,

the so-lauded **C. contraversa 'Variegata'** is wonderful in both shape and color (though not in the fall) but it really needs to stand by itself as it grows so wide, thus not really making a "companion."

A tree I would like to see grown more often has a great deal to offer. It is **Diospyros kaki** (Chinese persimmon, Japanese persimmon, kaki), a small tree with ornamental edible fruits that are a shiny bright orange. The fall leaf color is a startling orange-red, and since it has such large, lustrous leaves, this color is particularly vibrant. I strongly recommend it.

When I was a girl my mother grew laburnum, the variety called **Laburnum x watereri 'Vossii'**. This small tree is known as the golden rain tree because in late spring it has long racemes of bright yellow flowers. It is easy to grow and quite graceful. It may not be as commonly grown as it used to be because all its parts are poisonous, but so are many other plants such as rhododendrons and rhubarb leaves, which you would not dream of eating. My mother successfully raised five children and also nurtured a beautiful laburnum!

A very desirable North American tree that would look good anywhere but particularly so with acers, where it could show off and compare its fall color, is **Nyssa sylvatica** (black gum, sour gum, tupelo). It could be teamed with its Chinese cousin **N. sinensis** (Chinese tupelo), smaller growing and with possibly even brighter fall color in very bright red and orange. From Britain comes a selection called **'Sheffield Park'**, which has gold as well as red in its fall leaves. A very pretty semipendulous nyssa is **'Autumn Cascade'**. Nyssas do not much like being transplanted so it is best to buy small specimens and grow them where they are likely to stay for a long time.

Sometimes you have to be lucky. Some years ago I bought a small tree that I had never heard of but

Companion trees for maples

Species or cultivar	Height	Width	Zones
Cornus contraversa 'Variegata'	25 ft. (8 m)	25 ft. (8 m)	6–9
C. × 'Eddie's White Wonder'	20 ft. (6 m)	15 ft. (5 m)	5–8
C. florida	20 ft. (6 m)	25 ft. (8 m)	5–8
C. f. 'Cherokee Chief'	20 ft. (6 m)	25 ft. (8 m)	5–8
C. f. 'Cherokee Sunset'	20 ft. (6 m)	25 ft. (8 m)	5–8
C. kousa	22 ft. (7 m)	15 ft. (5 m)	5–8
C. k. 'Satomi'	22 ft. (7 m)	15 ft. (5 m)	5–8
Diospyros kaki	30 ft. (9 m)	22 ft. (7 m)	7–10
Laburnum × *watereri* 'Vossii'	25 ft. (8 m)	25 ft. (8 m)	6–8
Nyssa 'Autumn Cascade'	20 ft. (6 m)	20 ft. (6 m)	5–8
N. 'Sheffield Park'	25 ft. (8 m)	20 ft. (6 m)	5–8
N. sinensis	30 ft. (9 m)	30 ft. (9 m)	7–9
N. sylvatica	60 ft. (18 m)	30 ft. (9 m)	5–9
Pistacia chinensis	50–80 ft. (15–25 m)	22–30 ft. (7–9 m)	7–9
Sorbus 'Red Marbles'	24–36 ft. (7–12 m)	12 ft. (4 m)	5–8

which sounded interesting – and so it turned out to be. It is **Pistacia chinensis** (Chinese mastic), which has glossy green leaves and gorgeous fall color. It is related to *Rhus* (syn. *Toxicodendron*) and has pleasant, pale tan bark. It is quite narrow in shape so doesn't take up much room.

If you have read this far, you will have grasped that I am more than appreciative of fall color. I figure that if you are reading a book on maples you too will love a brilliant fall display. Therefore I feel that my last choice of companion tree will please. This is **Sorbus**, often called the rowan or mountain ash, a hardy tree that is not fussy about soil and will stand cold and wind. There are many varieties and they not only have vibrant fall color but wonderfully colored berries, too. What generosity! What is more, you may have a choice of color in these berries, including white. However, what is readily available is red, or pink and white. For real impact I like red, so I would choose a variety called **'Red Marbles'**,

Right: *Cornus* × 'Eddie's White Wonder'

which very reliably produces a wonderful crop of red fruit each year, much to the delight of the birds, not to mention the gardener.

Shrubs

I am going to start with one of my favorite garden subjects, the **mollis azalea hybrids.** This lovely shrub grows to about 6 ft. (2 m), offers wonderful, often warmly colored and strongly scented flowers before the appearance of fresh green leaves in spring, then wonderfully bright color before leaf fall. When I first grew these shrubs they were in very bright, hot colors of strong orange, yellow and red, which I thought most lively and cheerful. I still think so, but I have added some softer colors in white, pale lemon and apricot to my repertoire.

They are easy to grow in acidic soil but must have sun if they are to flower. This they do profusely, and nothing is prettier or sweeter smelling than a vase of them inside. As to choice, it is very wide so you may go to your garden center and choose while they are in flower. I will just mention a few that I have found particularly pleasing, not in any particular order of preference.

'Chelsea Reach' is a creamy semidouble with a pink outer layer, beautifully scented; 'Louie Williams' is scented soft pink with cream, and has an orange flare; 'Snowbird' has heaps of little scented white flowers and bluish leaves, and is just delicious; 'Yellow Beauty' is exactly that with an apricot flare. Then there is 'Eskimo Pie', which never fails to astonish people for it has large pure white flowers decorated with a yellow flare. The 'Melford' series, as in 'Melford Flame', 'Melford Gold', 'Melford Lemon' and 'Melford Yellow' are all very bright and striking in hot orange-reds and yellow. They are also beautifully fragrant with splendid fall color. There is no one who would not be enchanted with the double white, gorgeously fragrant 'Pavlova'. I also like two very attractive double, pale, scented plants, 'Taunton Glow' (pale yellow) and 'Taunton Lace' (cream and white).

Many of us have enjoyed growing the handsome camellia. As there is a midseason problem with petal blight I will just talk about the early-flowering *Camellia sasanqua*, which produces small, often fragrant flowers. Color and perfume together are a real blessing, but I will limit *C. sasanqua* to just one or two because it has a rather sprawling habit of growth. 'Mine-no-yuki' is a white, scented, peony form and 'Sparkling Burgundy' is a soft cerise-red with a lavender tinge.

A tough, easy-to-grow shrub is **Chaenomeles.** We used to call them "japonicas" and most gardens had one or two, quite often grown against a brick wall, which was a bit eye-searing since at one time you saw just the common orange. **C. japonica** (syn. *C. maulei*) (japonica, Japanese flowering quince) is an ornamental quince with wide saucer-shaped flowers and yellow fruits – and also thorns. These days you have a wide choice of colors in red, orange, pink, white and even a few bicolored. It makes a lovely cut flower and I think **C. speciosa 'Moerloosei'** (syn. 'Apple Blossom') (white, tinged pink), **C. s. 'Cardinalis'** (vivid red) and **C. x superba** (*C. japonica* x *C. speciosa*) **'Cameo'** (salmon and apricot) would make a very pleasant selection. Chaenomeles is so easy and accommodating to grow that you might like one or two more – perhaps **'Orange Flame'** (bright orange) or **'Green Ice'** (white, tinged green).

In the past, people grew vegetables and fruit among the flowers in cottage gardens, for the "cottages" were working people's homes, and as a rural wage was (and is) notoriously low, it was vital to grow food. We are not growing such gardens, but citrus fruits are so ornamental with shining green leaves, sweetly scented little white flowers and gorgeous, healthy, edible fruits that they would not be out of place as companions. I must mention here that citrus plants do not care for heavy frost so if you are colder than zone 8 they are not for you. These fruits like to be fed and watered, and if treated

The bright flowers of azalea mollis 'Melford Yellow' look striking against a backdrop of *Acer palmatum* var. *dissectum* 'Crimson Queen'.

well will reward you most handsomely. How about growing a **Citrus limon** (lemon), a **C. reticulata** (clementine, mandarin, tangerine) and a **C. sinensis 'Washington'** (sweet orange)? As these decorative fruits hang during the winter when color is at such a premium they really are valuable.

Corylopsis (winter hazel) is a relative of witch hazel and is very hardy. I am sorry that I do not see this shrub more often with its exquisitely beautiful racemes of bright yellow flowers in late winter and early spring. It spreads gracefully and is deciduous with quiet yellow leaves in fall. I am particularly pleased to have this winter-spring interest among my sleeping maples.

The shrub **Cotinus** (smoke bush) comes in various colors but the one I would select is called **C. coggygria 'Royal Purple'**. The reference to smoke

comes from the fact that the panicles of tiny flowers float above the plant in a sort of haze, looking ethereal above the sturdy bush. That is one reason to grow *Cotinus*; another is the stunning waxy, wine-red leaves, quite large, which turn orange and scarlet in the fall. These wonderful leaves look translucent in the sun.

You couldn't have nicer company than a daphne bush, grown particularly for its intense sweet perfume, its shining green leaves and neat habit. I suggest two: first **Daphne odora** (winter daphne), which flowers during winter and spring with little flowers in clusters. The variety *leucantha* is my choice, with white flowers blushed pink, its sweet perfume a real blessing in the winter garden. My other choice is the hybrid **D. x burkwoodii**, which flowers in late spring and early summer, so giving a lovely long season of perfume. Daphnes are not long-lived but it is not very expensive to replace them and they are worth it.

Deutzia are easy to grow and are cultivated for their late spring to early summer display of flowers. The branches arch gracefully and are smothered with flowers in mostly pink or white. It is necessary to prune them back after flowering, removing all the old wood and reducing the new branches a little. You would probably not die of despair if your maples were to be deprived of a deutzia to keep them company, but if you have space it is pleasant to have one or two. The best one I have is **'Magicien'**, lilac

pink, edged white, with a lilac-purple reverse. **'Pink Pompom'**, with double flowers in a soft rose pink, is well worth considering.

Enkianthus is one the loveliest shrubs, growing gracefully and rather slowly, its shape rather like a small tree. It has delicate, drooping flowers, cup- or urn-shaped with contrasting veins.

There are quite a few varieties but the one I know, and prize highly, is **E. *campanulatus*** (redvein enkianthus). Its flowers are pale yellow and red with darker veins. In the fall the leaves are brilliant in orange, red and yellow. Of the shrubs I

Enkianthus campanulatus

am recommending as companions this would be my first choice.

Eucryphia is a lovely evergreen shrub that I think deserves to be more widely grown, and which any self-respecting acer would like as a companion. *Eucryphia* is hardy and has mostly single white flowers, very like a camellia. It likes moist soil and is not fond of wind, making it very much at home with maples.

There are just five species in the genus, including **Eucryphia lucida** and **E. milliganii**, and then there is the hybrid **'Flora Plena'**, which, as its name suggests, has double white flowers. What is more, the charming flowers of these shrubs (or you might even consider them small trees) are fragrant. Those I have mentioned are quite readily available.

I have but one **Exochorda** and I have made a bit of a mess of growing this quite charming deciduous shrub. It is known as the pearlbush, and it has long, arching branches smothered in quite large white flowers. Where I went wrong was in not training the bush up by staking it, so that it would cascade down in the most appealing manner. However, my lower, rounded plant is still extremely pretty, and if you see one, buy it, for it has a good deal to offer.

Forsythia, the golden bell flower, has always been popular, for more than one reason. It is very easy and unfussy, and in the early spring it provides a sumptuous display of brilliant yellow flowers. **F. 'Beatrix Farrand'** is considered the best variety (developed at the Arnold Arboretum, Boston), because it has very large yellow flowers, a deeper color than the normal. All forsythia need trimming back after flowering. If you wish you could also have a hedge of forsythia.

One of my favorite shrubs for fall color, which looks very good below *Acer palmatum* and A. *japonica* in particular, is **Fothergilla**, hailing from North America. In spring it has bottlebrushlike flowers in

The leaf colors of *Fothergilla gardenii*, center, blend with the darker red of *Acer palmatum* var. *dissectum* 'Crimson Queen'.

cream, which you perhaps would not swoon over, but the fall is a different matter, when the quite large leaves put on an absolutely dazzling display in orange, red and purple. The two best varieties are the species itself, **F. major** (syn. *F. monticola*) and **F. gardenii** **'Blue Mist'**, which has lovely glaucous blue leaves that turn a gorgeous orange-red in fall.

Also from North America comes **Kalmia**, one of the most special and beautiful of shrubs. It is an evergreen, and in early summer has exquisite little cupped flowers in pink and white, or both, some with contrasting bands of color. It likes some sun but requires a moist, acidic soil. **K. latifolia** (calico bush, mountain laurel) has many beautiful cultivars, so it is just a matter of choosing. As usual, if you are not familiar with a subject but feel that you would like to

A white-flowered cultivar of *Viburnum*

know more about it, visit your garden center while the plant is flowering. I particularly like **'Sarah'**, a stunning red, and **'Pink Frost'**, but there are a good number from which to choose.

Yet again from the United States comes **Oxydendrum arboreum** (sorrel tree, sourwood). Although it has white flowers in panicles rather like a *Pieris*, it is really grown for its astonishing fall color of crimson and yellow, said to be one of the very best subjects for fall display. I am not sure just how available this desirable shrub is but I do know that it likes a cool root run and a cool climate.

You really should not be without one **Philadelphus** (mock orange). It is so easy to grow, with beautifully fragrant white flowers. The only catch is that it does not like acidic soil, which I have. Having said that, *Philadelphus* grows quite happily here, which seems odd when all the authorities say it is a lime lover. Perhaps they mean that it grows better in calcareous soils. There are quite a number of varieties from which to choose, but just remember that when they have flowered, it is necessary to prune them back so that they do not grow too leggy.

My mother grew something she called "sumach" and it was many years before I realized that this was **Rhus** (syn. *Toxicodendron*), or sumac. The best one is probably **R. typhina 'Dissecta'** (syn. 'Laciniata'), which has incised leaves that look rather fernlike, with vivid orange and red fall colors. It has flowers, too, that produce red berries. We did not ever have any ill effects from my mother's "sumach," but the sap of some species is an irritant. Perhaps her children did not go around with an ax, lopping off branches. Rhus, however, is most decorative and striking in fall, and if you have the space is well worth growing.

Should you want to grow **Stachyurus praecox** (and having seen it, I am sure you would love to have it), give it a good deal of lateral room. It is a really beautiful Japanese shrub, which is also very generous. In late winter and early spring it displays long, drooping racemes of cup-shaped, pale yellow-green flowers. It then has quite large heart-shaped leaves that color quietly in the fall in yellow tinged with pink. One of its glories is its graceful branching, which spreads wide, showing polished brown in color. It is lovely, easy to grow and readily available, making a splendid companion for almost anything.

Stewartia (syn. *Stuartia*) is a close cousin of the camellia and unfortunately is not grown widely enough. It has pure white flowers, produced in summer. When the shrub is older it has a most attractive peeling bark, and fall color of red and yellow. The best garden variety is probably **S. pseudocamellia Koreana Group** (syn. S. *koreana*, S. *pseudocamellia* var. *koreana*) because its flowers are particularly large and its fall color particularly bright.

The last shrub I am going to mention as a companion for maples is certainly not the least. This is the **Viburnum**, which has a bewildering number of species and hybrids. This is of no great concern because only two or three with wonderful perfume are necessary. Although they have many other architectural uses, it is its perfume, at least for me, which makes the viburnum so attractive.

This shrub is very simple to grow, not being particular about soil and needing little attention except an occasional trim. You may have evergreen versions, or some that are grown particularly for their berries – the choice is yours. However, I suggest some spring-flowering varieties with the most glorious fragrance. These are **Viburnum x burkwoodii 'Anne Russell'** (V. *carlesii* x V. *utite*), which has white flowers; **'Aurora'**, which is pink; and **V. x burkwoodi 'Fulbrook'** which has pink buds and white flowers. On cool spring days the perfume wafts though the garden, beautifully sweet.

Perennials

I have discussed trees and shrubs as companions for acers at some length, and it is time to discuss what might be called the "bottom story." You can use almost anything in the way of perennials, but I will suggest some personal favorites that I have found most satisfactory, both for beauty and ease of cultivation.

The choice of perennials is very wide. However, as we are planting under deciduous trees, which give dappled shade, our choice of perennials is limited to those that will thrive in these conditions. Since deciduous trees lose their leaves, the winter sun has a therapeutic effect on the soil; the fallen leaves make a beautiful mulch, while in summer the dappled shade creates a very favorable environment.

However, most perennials like soil that does not dry out, and in dry periods it will be necessary to apply water. In these days of handy, inexpensive watering systems it is a good investment to buy one, even if you use it only infrequently.

Aruncus dioicus (syn. A. *sylvester*, *Spiraea aruncus*), or goatsbeard, is a stately plant with fernlike green foliage and huge graceful plumes of creamy white flowers. It is a fitting plant to begin this list of desirable perennials for underplanting maples.

Brunnera macrophylla (syn. *Anchusa myosotidiflora*), or Siberian bugloss, is a sort of aristocratic forget-me-not with large heart-shaped hairy leaves, topped by airy panicles of dainty blue flowers. It is a very satisfactory plant, but I have not found the variegated form with green leaves splashed and edged white so easy. It is called **'Dawson's White'** and seems a bit touchy and not so robust.

From North America comes **Disporum** (fairy bells). It has lance-shaped leaves and cream flowers. My version is **D. sessile 'Variegatum'** and it is a good buy because where you had one, you will soon have 50. I do not find this a problem because it is quite

Companion shrubs for maples

Species or cultivar	Height	Width	Zones
Camellia sasanqua	20 ft. (6 m)	12 ft. (4 m)	6–8
C. s. 'Mine-no-yuki'	20 ft. (6 m)	10 ft. (3 m)	7–8
C. s. 'Sparkling Burgundy'	5–10 ft. (1.5–3 m)	3–6 ft. (1–2 m)	7–8
Chaenomeles japonica	3 ft. (1 m)	6 ft. (2 m)	5–9
C. speciosa 'Cardinalis'	8 ft. (2.5 m)	15 ft. (5 m)	5–8
C. s. 'Moerloosei'	8 ft. (2.5 m)	15 ft. (5 m)	5–8
C. x superba 'Cameo'	5 ft. (1.5 m)	6 ft. (2 m)	5–9
Citrus limon	6–22 ft. (2–7 m)	5–10 ft. (1.5–3 m)	min. 37–41°F (3–5°C)
C. reticulata	6–22 ft. (2–7 m)	5–10 ft. (1.5–3 m)	min. 37–41°F (3–5°C)
C. sinensis 'Washington'	20–40 ft. (6–12 m)	10–15 ft. (3–5 m)	min. 37–41°F (3–5°C)
Corylopsis	12 ft. (4 m)	9 ft. (2.7 m)	7–9
Cotinus	15 ft. (5 m)	15 ft. (5 m)	5–8
Daphne odora	3 ft. (1 m)	3 ft. (1 m)	6–9
D. o. var. leucantha	4 ft. (1.2 m)	4 ft. (1.2 m)	7–9
D. x burkwoodii	3–5 ft. (1–1.5 m)	3–5 ft. (1–1.5 m)	5–8
Deutzia 'Magicien'	5 ft. (1.5 m)	5 ft. (1.5 m)	6–8
D. 'Pink Pompom'	5 ft. (1.5 m)	5 ft. (1.5 m)	6–8
Enkianthus campanulatus	12–15 ft. (4–5 m)	12–15 ft. (4–5 m)	5–8
Eucryphia 'Flora Plena'	20 ft. (6 m)	15 ft. (5 m)	9–10
E. lucida	25 ft. (8 m)	12 ft. (4 m)	9–10
E. milliganii	20 ft. (6 m)	5 ft. (1.5 m)	8–9
Exochorda	5 ft. (1.5 m)	6 ft. (2 m)	6–9
Forsythia 'Beatrix Farrand'	6 ft. (2 m)	6 ft. (2 m)	6–9
Fothergilla major	8 ft. (2.5 m)	6 ft. (2 m)	5–8
F. gardenii 'Blue Mist'	3 ft. (1 m)	3 ft. (1 m)	5–9

easily removed if you do not want it, but a clump does make an impact.

Epimedium (barrenwort) is grown mainly for its pretty leaves, though its small flowers are most attractive. The leaves are ovate. In the commonly grown form **E. pinnatum** the little flowers are yellow. I have also a form with coppery colored flowers and streaked reddish leaves, **E. x rubrum** (*E. alpinum* x *E. grandiflorum*), which is just lovely. These plants like semishade and are discreet rather than spectacular, but pleasant and trouble-free.

Eupatorium (hemp agrimony), particularly **E. rugosum** (syn. *E. urticifolium*), is known as white snakeroot and has coarse leaves and clouds of white flowers. Another version is called **'Chocolate'** and has dark foliage with white flowers.

Helleborus* x *orientalis (Lenten rose) has beautiful open, cup-shaped flowers in attractive white, soft pink, maroon and red, spotted or marbled in contrasting colors. I particularly love the boss of central stamens like a little crown. These plants are evergreen but the old leaves can be a bit unsightly,

Species or cultivar	Height	Width	Zones
Kalmia latifolia f. *myrtifolia*			
'Sarah'	4 ft. (1.2 m)	4 ft. (1.2 m)	5–9
'Pink Frost'	5 ft. (1.5 m)	3 ft. (1 m)	5–9
Oxydendrum arboreum	30–50 ft. (10–15 m)	25 ft. (8 m)	5–9
Philadelphus	6 ft. (2 m)	5 ft. (1.5 m)	4–9
Rhododendron (mollis azaleas)			
'Chelsea Reach'	6 ft. (2 m)	4 ft. (1.2 m)	6–9
'Eskimo Pie'	6 ft. (2 m)	4 ft. (1.2 m)	6–9
'Louie Williams'	6 ft. (2 m)	4 ft. (1.2 m)	6–9
'Melford Flame'	6 ft. (2 m)	4 ft. (1.2 m)	6–9
'Melford Gold'	6 ft. (2 m)	4 ft. (1.2 m)	6–9
'Melford Lemon'	6 ft. (2 m)	4 ft. (1.2 m)	6–9
'Pavlova'	6 ft. (2 m)	4 ft. (1.2 m)	6–9
'Snowbird'	6 ft. (2 m)	4 ft. (1.2 m)	6–9
'Taunton Glow'	6 ft. (2 m)	4 ft. (1.2 m)	6–9
'Taunton Lace'	6 ft. (2 m)	4 ft. (1.2 m)	6–9
'Melford Yellow'	6 ft. (2 m)	4 ft. (1.2 m)	6–9
'Yellow Beauty'	6 ft. (2 m)	4 ft. (1.2 m)	6–9
Rhus typhina 'Dissecta'	6 ft. (2 m)	10 ft. (3 m)	3–8
Stachyurus praecox	3–12 ft. (1–4 m)	10 ft. (3 m)	7–9
Stewartia pseudocamellia			
Koreana Group	70 ft. (20 m)	25 ft. (8 m)	5–8
Viburnum × *burkwoodii*			
'Anne Russell'	6 ft. (2 m)	5 ft. (1.5 m)	4–8
'Aurora'	6 ft. (2 m)	3 ft. (1 m)	4–8
'Fulbrook'	8 ft. (2.5 m)	8 ft. (2.5 m)	4–8

so it pays to cut them off in fall; then feed the plants and – lo and behold – in the late winter–early spring the flowers stand proudly and can be easily observed because there are no old leathery leaves in the way.

A North American perennial of great merit and diversity of color is **Heuchera** (coral flower). This plant has low clumps of leaves with panicles of flowers, bell-shaped in reds, creams, pink or yellow. Since this plant has become popular, many new cultivars have appeared so that now leaves are not merely green, but come in wondrous shades of purple (**'Plum Pudding'**, **'Purple Petticoats'**), green and silver (**'Amethyst Myst'**, **'Mint Frost'**), silver and lavender (**'Regal Rose'**) and gray-bronze (**'Smokey Rose'**). Then to cap it all off, crosses have been made between *Tiarella* and *Heuchera*, giving a plant that many think outshines its parents. **'Silver Streak'** has purple leaves infused with silver and cream flowers, whereas **'Viking Ship'** I have only read about, but it does sound splendid. It has silvery leaves with detached leaflets that apparently look like little oars! I gather that in the summer the leaves fill in.

The weeping Japanese maple *Acer palmatum* 'Crimson Queen' underplanted with hellebores

The **Hosta** (plantain lily) is the perfect perennial, very diverse as to leaf form and color, rejoicing in filtered shade, both easy and rewarding to grow. As hostas are so immensely popular, much work has gone into hybridizing, so the choice is extensive. A visit to your garden center in the spring will allow you to choose from a good number of varieties. Hostas are grown for their beautiful leaves, but they have flowers in early summer in mainly lavender or blue, though some are white.

Polygonatum x hybridum, commonly known as Solomon's seal, is just lovely with its arching stems of green-tipped, white bells. It will grow most anywhere but looks particularly good under trees, is very hardy and spreads quite satisfactorily.

Polygonatum x *hybridum* is the common garden plant and is highly recommended.

Pulmonaria (lungwort) always sounds to me a bit like a respiratory disease, but it is actually a low-growing perennial with rough leaves, very often speckled or splashed with white, which likes to grow in dappled shade. It has pretty flowers, which stand above the leaves, in blue, pink, red or white. It is hardy, attractive and easy to grow so is becoming increasingly popular. There are both species and hybrids from which to choose.

From North America comes a dear little plant called **Tiarella** with heart-shaped leaves that turn reddish in fall and above them spikes of creamy white

Above: Hostas and epimediums underneath a small *Acer palmatum* var. *dissectum*

Left: The maple *Acer palmatum* var. *dissectum* 'Filigree' planted next to hostas and dicentras

flowers. Its common name of foam flower gives a good idea as to how the blooms look. As the clumps spread, the plants make quite an impact, though always in quiet good taste.

Bulbs

I have discussed many maples and mentioned trees, shrubs and perennials as suitable companions. There is but one "layer" left and that is the very "ground floor," so to speak. Dappled shade with sunny edges has been created, so this will need to be considered when choosing what might be considered the finishing touches. When choosing bulbs, I would not ignore bluebells and daffodils, so essentially spring. The bluebells are happy in shade, but have the daffodils at the front because they love sun.

Most bulbs would be suitable for underplanting maples, but I will just mention some that are not difficult to grow in any soil that does not dry out. To make sure the soil stays nicely moist add your favorite mulch. Compost, leaf mold or mushroom compost are all good options.

I could not possibly overlook what is universally known as naked ladies, **Amaryllis belladonna** (magic lily, resurrection lily). The flowers come in late summer on long, sturdy stems with clusters of sweetly scented trumpets at the top. They give the impression of shooting up out of nothing because the foliage appears later. The color most commonly seen is pink, but there are versions in white and a rather attractive cerise. These bulbs need a warm place to flower really well.

Arisaema are my latest craze and I cannot recommend them highly enough for their faintly sinister beauty. They have hooded flowers called spathes and a sort of pencil up the middle called a spadix.

The word "exotic" was surely coined for these strangely beautiful plants. They prefer dappled shade, so are splendid among deciduous trees like maples. Some are soft green; some are striped in green, purple or black; all are fascinating. They are

Companion perennials for maples

Species or cultivar	Height	Width	Zones
Aruncus dioicus	6 ft. (2 m)	4 ft. (1.2 m)	3–7
Brunnera macrophylla	18 in. (45 cm)	24 in. (60 cm)	3–7
B. m. 'Dawson's White'	18 in. (45 cm)	24 in. (60 cm)	3–7
Disporum sessile	24 in. (60 cm)	24 in. (60 cm)	4–9
D. s. 'Variegatum'	18 in. (45 cm)	36 in. (90 cm)	4–9
Epimedium pinnatum	8–12 in. (20–30 cm)	8–12 in. (20–30 cm)	5–9
E. × *rubrum*	12 in. (30 cm)	12 in. (30 cm)	4–8
Eupatorium rugosum	5–6 ft. (1.5–2 m)	24 in. (60 cm)	4–9
Helleborus × *orientalis*	to 18 in. (45 cm)	to 18 in. (45 cm)	4–9
Heuchera	8 in. (20 cm)	8 in. (20 cm)	4–9
H. 'Amethyst Myst'	8 in. (20 cm)	8 in. (20 cm)	4–9
H. 'Mint Frost'	8 in. (20 cm)	8 in. (20 cm)	4–9
H. 'Plum Pudding'	8 in. (20 cm)	8 in. (20 cm)	4–9
H. 'Purple Petticoats'	8 in. (20 cm)	8 in. (20 cm)	4–9
H. 'Regal Rose'	8 in. (20 cm)	8 in. (20 cm)	4–9
H. 'Silver Streak'	8 in. (20 cm)	8 in. (20 cm)	4–9
H. 'Smokey Rose'	8 in. (20 cm)	8 in. (20 cm)	4–9
H. 'Viking Ship'	8 in. (20 cm)	8 in. (20 cm)	4–9
Hosta	size depends on cultivar selected		3–8
Polygonatum × *hybridum*	36 in. (90 cm)	12 in. (30 cm)	4–9
Pulmonaria	10–16 in. (25–40 cm)	18–24 in. (45–60 cm)	5–8
Tiarella	13 in. (35 cm)	13 in. (35 cm)	4–9

not difficult to grow in partial shade in humus-rich soil that does not dry out.

Arisaema are becoming more readily available. **A. tortuosum** (syn. *A. helleborifolium*) has green flowers with a long, twisted spadix (I guess this is the "tortured" bit). I was astonished when mine reached a height of 3 ft. (1 m). I bought them as babies and they soon flowered, but every year they have grown bigger till now they are quite magnificent. In the fall they sport bright orange seeds, and little seedlings are popping up here and there without any help from me.

Another recommended *Arisaema* is **A. candidissimum**, which has enormous leaves and a pink and white striped flower. It is very fetching indeed, and because of its pretty coloring does not look at all sinister.

From North America come **Camassia** (quamash), members of the hyacinth family. They grow quite tall with narrow, erect spikes of flowers. **C. leichtlinii** is a pretty blue-lilac and **'Alba'** is white. They look best planted in groups. Camassias have the odd habit of burying themselves deeper and deeper, so every now and then you must lift them and replant, otherwise they will stop flowering.

Nobody could resist the Himalayan lily **Cardiocrinum giganteum**, which needs shade and moist soil. It is quite the most spectacular bulb, with fragrant, pendent, trumpet-shaped flowers in cream with red stripes. It takes years to flower but once it does it produces copious seeds, themselves a feature for they stand on lancelike stems for many months. The mother bulb has bulblets, which will flower in due course. Once you have *Cardiocrinum* to flowering size you seem to get a succession. The large, shining, heart-shaped leaves are a feature in themselves, rivaling the biggest hostas. The perfume is heavenly

Right: Daffodils, one of the essential bulbs of spring, work well underneath maples.

and can be enjoyed from a distance, for it seems to waft a long way.

Another delightful lilylike bulb is **Crinum**. It has large, beautiful, fragrant, funnel-shaped flowers and huge bulbs. There are a great number of species and hybrids, but the one most commonly grown is **C. moorei** with large bell-shaped flowers in pale pink with a lovely pervasive perfume. Then there is the hybrid **C. x powillii** (*C. bulbispermum* x *C. moorei*), which is considered a very good landscaping plant; it is not too fussy if the soil is damp or dry, but it likes some shade.

Nothing is happier under deciduous trees than the delectable little woodland **Cyclamen** with their prettily mottled leaves and perky little flowers in pink, white or cerise. If you purchase different species you may have cyclamens flowering most of the year. When I am a very old lady I am definitely going to have a raised bed of these favorite bulbs. **C. coum** flowers in winter through to spring, while **C. hederifolium** flowers in the fall.

Erythronium, Fritallaria and *Trillium* (trinity flower, wakerobin, wood lily) would all be happy under maples and would be difficult to beat for sheer delicate beauty. Any cultivars of these lovely bulbs would delight you.

Companion bulbs for maples

Species or cultivar	Height	Zones
Amaryllis belladonna	24 in. (60 cm)	7–10
Arisaema	(depends on the species)	(depends on the species)
A. tortuosum	5 ft. (1.5 m)	8–9
A. candidissimum	16 in. (40 cm)	6–9
Camassia leichtlinii	2–4½ ft. (0.5–1.3 m)	4–10
C. l. 'Alba'	4 ft. (1.2 m)	4–10
Cardiocrinum giganteum	5–12 ft. (1.5–4 m)	7–9
Crinum moorei	24 in. (60 cm)	7–9
C. × powillii	5 ft. (1.5 m)	7–10
Cyclamen	6 in. (15 cm)	4–9
Erythronium	6 in. (15 cm)	4–8
Fritallaria	12 in. (30 cm)	6–9
Galtonia candicans	3–4 ft. (1–1.2 m)	7–10
Nomocharis	3 ft. (1 m)	4–8
Trillium	12 in. (30 cm)	4–8

Galtonia is a summer-flowering bulb. As so many plants flower in the spring these summer-flowering plants make a valuable contribution by brightening up surrounding greens. **G. candicans** is sometimes called a summer hyacinth, though it does not look much like the stubby, forced, multiflowered heads so common in bowls on the coffee table. It has tall, unbranched stems hung with white scented bells, and looks striking in a group. It seeds readily but if too wet in winter the bulbs can rot.

Most of these bulbs are quite tall, so it would be nice to plant some little treasures where there is a suitable spot.

Nomocharis is a pretty plant that is not perhaps very well-known. It is a bit like a loose-limbed lily with flat, mostly pink flowers, which are heavily spotted and have a dark eye. It flowers in the summer and likes some shade. **N. pardonthina** is the most commonly grown.

Opposite: Maples *Acer palmatum* var. *dissectum* and *Acer palmatum* 'Shin-deshojo' underplanted with bluebells

These bulbs and, in fact, all bulbs, are wonderful garden subjects. They do not come cheaply, but against that they mostly increase quite rapidly so your original investment soon shows dividends.

Above: The pretty *Cyclamen coum* can look very good with a suitably small and delicate maple.

CHAPTER 8

Landscaping with Maples in Containers

Modern gardens, on the whole, are very much smaller than they were even 20 years ago, but despite space restrictions, many gardeners wish to grow a wide selection of plants. One way of overcoming lack of space is to use containers, which now have a culture all their own.

The art of container gardening is not a new concept, but with the increase in recent years of smaller gardens, it has become much more innovative and adventurous. From a practical point of view, containers utilize what could be termed "waste space" – the paving or concrete surrounding a house. Some infill housing might have no garden space at all, just some paving, so to soften the environment container plants are the only option.

In addition, many people cannot (or do not want to) spend time "gardening," but find that planting and looking after containers is not too onerous, and the return in providing a pleasant environment is gratifying. A side benefit is that, should you move from one house to another, you do not have to leave all your carefully nurtured plants behind. It is all very well being altruistic and thinking that the new owner will love your garden, but this unselfish view scarcely compensates for the loss of plants you have looked after for years. With containers you just pack them up and take them with you and they provide at least the nucleus of a garden at your new place. Planting maples in containers also allows gardeners

Opposite: The little red weeping Japanese maple 'Ever Red'

Acer palmatum var. *dissectum* 'Crimson Queen'

in cold climates, of zones 4 and below, to grow and enjoy the less hardy maple species (see Chapter 1, page 13).

Many people plant bright, showy flowers, often annuals, which look cheerful. To complement these sorts of containers we may have some that grow in beauty with the years, providing structure, shape and grace for a long time. This is where small-growing and weeping maples are absolutely ideal.

Container-grown weeping or dwarf maples look superb. With the help of a trolley, the containers may be moved strategically around the garden, or you can simply choose a permanent place and enjoy their beauty every day. As you have to water containers frequently, at least during the summer, you are able to study the seasonal changes more closely. This aspect in itself can provide the container gardener with a great deal of pleasure.

To successfully grow a plant in a container you need to learn some basic concepts. What you are doing is persuading a plant to live and flourish in an environment that is not natural to it. In the garden, the plant gets nutrients from the soil, and moisture from rain (at least most of the time). It is vastly different in a container where the plant waits anxiously for you to water and feed it, for it is very dependent upon you.

First you have to provide a suitable container. Choose one that is big enough, for you are better to have just one tree in an adequately sized container than you are to have two whose containers will soon be outgrown. Also it is false economy to buy cheap containers as their lifespan is usually short.

Having chosen your containers, the next thing is adequate drainage. Choose a container with a drainage hole or holes. My preferred method is to use pieces of broken containers or stones in the bottom of the pot to provide air pockets that allow excess water to drain out, as sometimes the drainage holes can get clogged up with soil mix. It is also a good idea to place the container on a free-draining medium, such as sand or soil, rather than concrete or a flat paving stone. Alternatively, you could raise the containers a little above the ground, which also facilitates water drainage.

After this, fill the container with a good mix from your local garden center. You may make your own mix but it is very much simpler to buy a scientifically mixed medium. These mixes also have the advantage of being free-draining if they are a good quality container mix. This means that you can get away without using the crockery/stone layer described above, as the mix will not clog the drainage holes in the pot.

You can now plant your tree, carefully spreading out the roots at the base of the rootball. Water it

Above: *Acer palmatum* 'Chishio'
Left: A slightly larger maple, in this case *Acer palmatum* 'Beni-komachi', in a container

well. I like to add a layer of compost, and once a year give it some slow-release fertilizer (10-10-10).

During summer you will need to water frequently, and probably not at all in winter. Your own judgment and experience will tell you when this is necessary, but the golden rule is never to let your containers dry out.

The choice of maples to grow in containers is simple: any or all of *Acer palmatum* var. *dissectum*. There are also some small-growing or dwarf upright maples, which would look very good in containers.

Having planted containers with some favorite maples, the next consideration is where to place them. Do not put them where strong winds blow. They might not actually die if living in a howling gale but they would certainly be tattered and unattractive. However, I would not place them hard against a hot wall either.

Containers add great interest either when placed strategically in the garden or on concrete. They can hide areas that are not desirable and may be grouped to make a garden in themselves. Potted maples would make splendid feature plants at your entrance or front door. In fact, there are probably as many ways to use these maples as your imagination can encompass, knowing that however you place them they will look beautiful and provide you with endless pleasure.

The art of bonsai

Bonsai is the growing of trees and shrubs in small containers so that they do not attain full size. Anyone can plant a container and have it look good, but bonsai is an art.

It is thought to have originated in China 1,500 years ago, but the oldest evidence of bonsai is Japanese, shown in a scroll painting 800 years old. Whether it started in Japan or not, this art form is now firmly Japanese.

What is the rationale behind what we might think of as stunting trees? The Japanese are known for their deep appreciation of beauty and form. Many have very little land available for cultivation or gardening, and a great number of people have an abiding love of the natural world. They have cleverly adapted to these circumstances by making gardens in miniature!

In the beginning, wealthy Japanese collected naturally dwarfed trees in the wild, but the supply was soon exhausted, so artificial dwarfing was the logical next step. Next came the sophisticated art of pruning.

The tree is not supposed to look exactly as it would in the wild, albeit in miniature. Rather it has a spiritual content that the artists' skill for balance

Above left: *Acer palmatum* 'Kamagata' brilliantly complemented by the dark doors
Left: *Acer palmatum atropurpureum* lifted above the daises by its container

Maples make wonderful subjects for bonsai.

and line evokes. From just one plant can come a feeling not only of peace but of the spirit of nature.

This might sound daunting for those of us not steeped in Japanese culture, but, as with many other aspects of life, if you really want to do something, it is necessary to study it. The best way to do this is to join a club, observe how trees grow naturally, and look at illustrations of bonsai in textbooks.

Acer palmatum make splendid subjects for bonsai, the classic species being A. *buergerianum* and A. *palmatum*. However, many other maples have been found suitable including A. *japonicum*, A. *campestre*, A. *ginnala*, A. *griseum* and A. *rubrum*.

Although you might think that bonsai trees have to be very old, that is not so. From what I understand, the art is to make the little tree look venerable and there are interesting techniques that produce this effect. I think that bonsai is something that you either have a real affinity for and appreciation of the skill involved, or you are indifferent.

For those who are truly interested, it is an absorbing hobby about which you can learn all the time, and produce for your efforts a tree of great beauty that could well live 100 years after you have gone.

Epilogue

Sometimes I think about what plants I will just have to have when age forces me to leave my large garden where I have space to plant most of what I want. If there isn't room here for something new, I just throw out a poor performer.

What maples would I take if I had restricted space? When it comes to choosing just 20 or so maples the decision will be most difficult and agonizing. I hope that I will have a garden large enough to take even that small number.

Japanese maples are my very particular favorites. As well as being stunningly beautiful, they are small trees, which will no doubt influence my choice to some extent.

So, right now, this is how I see my choices – with the proviso that I could have to juggle a little if something astonishingly beautiful should suddenly appear on the market!

Acer palmatum 'Beni-komachi' and 'Beni-maiko' are rather similar in their stunning colors, such a brilliant scarlet-pink in spring, but I shall have to have them both – after all, they are small-growing so will take up little space.

The next choices are also bright: 'Okagami', dark red in spring, shouting scarlet in fall; 'Shin-deshojo', scarlet pink changing over spring until brilliant in fall; and 'Beni-otake' with narrow bamboolike leaves, scarlet and then red.

'Katsura' is harbinger of spring for maples in my garden, the first to come out in its beautiful soft

Acer palmatum 'Kamagata'

golden-orange leaves, which make a lovely contrast in fall, for its leaves turn yellow.

For green I would choose 'Lutescens', which is not as common as it should be. It is yellow-green, soon turning green in spring, then a lovely deep yellow in fall.

I see I am racing through my choices before I have considered anything other than *Acer palmatum*. For *A. palmatum* var. *dissectum* any or all would be simply splendid – and this only uses up one choice.

So what next? I think it will have to be *Acer japonicum* 'Aconitifolium' for its very large, deeply divided, quite stiff-looking leaves, and most of all for its astonishing orange and scarlet fall foliage.

Opposite: Looking through hostas and other perennials to red and green Japanese maples.

I would feel very deprived if I could not have *Acer davidii* with its striped bark, pretty flowers, handsome shiny leaves and beautiful fall color.

Acer rubrum, from North America, is splendid but it is also very large, so although maybe I cannot have my favorite A. *rubrum* 'October Glory', I am going to have A. x *freemanii* because it is a hybrid between A. *rubrum* and A. *saccharinum*. The best of both worlds is always an attractive maxim and that is what I will have when I choose A. x *freemanii* 'Autumn Blaze', so very well named.

Some people consider my next choice, *Acer griseum*, the most splendid of all maples. I do not go as far as that, but I certainly rate it very highly. Because of its wonderful dark brown peeling bark and small trifoliate leaves, orange-yellow in fall, it is not like any other maple. I find that it likes quite a lot of shade, so is splendid in woodland conditions. As it is appallingly difficult to propagate, A. *griseum* does not flood the market, but may be purchased (sometimes) from good garden centers.

My next choice is a maple I have not yet seen but it sounds so wonderful in description that I hanker after it. *Acer pensylvanicum* is another from North America, and I want it particularly because it has the most striking striped bark of any maple, and would be very rewarding to study in winter when the bark is a reddish color with very distinctive wide, white stripes. The fall color is brilliant gold. It does not have many cultivars, and they may be difficult to source.

Acer platanoides, commonly known as the Norway maple, has many cultivars, but I shall settle for 'Crimson King', such a splendid tree for

Acer palmatum 'Beni-otake'

Above: *Acer palmatum* 'Toyama-nishiki'
Right: *Acer palmatum* 'Seiryu' with *Acer palmatum* var.
dissectum 'Crimson Queen' in the foreground

its lovely red coloring in both spring and fall. A North American selection called 'Crimson Sentry' is smaller-growing but equally fine in color.

You would not believe just how many cultivars of *Acer pseudoplatanus* there are, and how very beautiful some of them are, but I shall limit myself to just two. The first is 'Brilliantissimum' with orange-yellow leaves in spring, growing very slowly. Actually, it is a bit of a challenge for it really must have quite a lot of shade; hot sun makes a real mess of its leaves. If you are able to give it a suitable habitat it will be very rewarding – delicately beautiful – not in the least like the rumbustious species. The New Zealand raised 'Esk Sunset' is worthy of a place in any garden because of its beautiful pink, green and mahogany coloring. It is also slow-growing.

You might think that my next choice, *Acer shirasawanum* 'Autumn Moon', would need to be

tucked in some nicely sheltered place, but not so. This beautifully colored tree, in a sort of pale rusty orange, rejoices in sun. Too much shade would bleach its delicate coloring.

I will certainly have to have a cultivar of the sugar maple of North America for its wonderful fall colors. There are lots to choose from, but *Acer saccharum*

'Bonfire' will suit very well. From North America also comes *Acer negundo*, the box elder. The variety I grow and regard highly is *A. n.* 'Flamingo' because in spring its green leaves are margined a distinct pink, later turning to white, and very pretty it is, too. From New Zealand comes 'Kelly's Gold' with soft yellow foliage.

Many years ago I first saw *Acer buergerianum*. I could not believe its beautiful fall color, the most gorgeous orange, yellow and red. I bought it on the spot, and was delighted to find it lovely in spring also, so I shall certainly always have to grow it. As I write I can see it, growing very fast and absolutely trouble-free.

These are the acers that I would most like to take to my new home, if I had to restrict my choice to just a few.

APPENDIX

Sources of Maples in North America

The importation of live plants and plant materials across borders requires special arrangements, which will be detailed in suppliers' catalogs. Americans must have a permit, obtained through the Web site given below. Every order requires a phytosanitary certificate supplied by the exporter, and purchasers should verify this at the time of order. (If certain plants are exempt from this certificate, the seller will know.)

A CITES (Convention on International Trade in Endangered Species of Wild Fauna and Flora) certificate may also be required if the plant is an endangered species. For more information contact:
USDA-APHIS-PPQ
Permit Unit
4700 River Road, Unit 136
Riverdale, MD 20727-1236
Ph: (301) 734-8645. Fax: (301) 734-5786
www.aphis.usda.gov

Canadians importing plant material must pay a fee and complete an "application for permit to import." A phytosanitary certificate may also be required. For more information contact:
Plant Health and Production Division
Canadian Food Inspection Agency
2nd Floor West, Permit Office
59 Camelot Drive
Nepean, ON K1A 0Y9
Ph: (613) 225-2342. Fax: (613) 228-6605
www.inspection.gc.ca

Aesthetic Gardens
P.O. Box 1362
Boring, OR 97009
Fax: (503) 663-6672
www.agardens.com

Bloom River Gardens
P.O. Box 177
Walterville, OR 97489
Tel: (541) 726-8997. Fax: (541) 726-4052
E-mail: plants@bloomriver.com
www.bloomriver.com

Eastwoods Nurseries
634 Long Mountain Road
Washington, VA 22747
Tel: (540) 675-1234
E-mail: maples@japanesemaples.com
www.japanesemaples.com

Forestfarm
990 Tetherow Road
Williams, OR 97544-9599
Tel: (541) 846-7269. Fax: (541) 846-6963
E-mail: plants@forestfarm.com
www.forestfarm.com

Fraser's Thimble Farms
175 Arbutus Road
Salt Spring Island, BC V8K 1A3
Tel: (250) 537-5788. Fax: (250) 537-5788
www.thimblefarms.com

Heronswood Nursery
7530 NE 288th St.
Kingston, WA 98346
Tel: (360) 297-4172. Fax: (360) 297-8321
E-mail: info@heronswood.com
www.heronswood.com

Mountain Maples
Mendocino, CA
Tel: (707) 743-1314, (888) 707-6522
Fax: (707) 984-7433
www.mountainmaples.com

Peninsula Flowers Nursery
8512 West Saanich Road
Sidney, BC V8L 5W1
Tel: (250) 652-9602. Fax: (250) 652-9602
E-mail: bonsaibc@shaw.ca
www.bonsaobc.ca

Variegated Foliage Nursery
245 Westford Road
Eastford, CT 06242
Tel: (860) 974-3951. Fax: (860) 974-3951
www.variegatedfolige.com

Wildwood Farm
10300 Sonoma Highway
Kenwood, CA 95452
Tel: (707) 833-1161, (888) 833-4181
Fax: (415) 453-9070
www.wildwoodmaples.com

Bibliography

Harris, James G.S. *The Gardener's Guide to Growing Maples.* Hawthorne, Victoria: Blooming Books, 2000.

Hutchinson, Colin. *The Art of Gardening.* Auckland: Whitcoulls/Palmers Gardenworld, 1992.

The Hillier Manual of Trees and Shrubs. (6th ed.) Newton Abbott: David & Charles Ltd., 1991.

van Gelderen, D.M., de Jong, P.C, Oterdoom, H.J. *Maples of the World.* Portland, Oregon: Timber Press, 1994.

Vertrees, J.D. *Japanese Maples.* Portland, Oregon: Timber Press, 1978.

Index

Numbers in bold indicate an illustration.

Acer acuminatum 49
Acer buergerianum 13, 37, **38**, 87, 92
  'Goshiki-kaede' 37
Acer campestre 49, 87
  'Carnival' 49
  'Postelense' 49
  'Pulverulentum' 49
Acer cappadocicum 49, 62
  'Aureum' 49, 62
  'Rubrum' 49, 62
Acer cappadocicum var. mono 40
Acer circinatum 43, 60
  'Little Gem' 43, 60
  'Monroe' 43
Acer x conspicuum 49
  'Elephant's Ear' 49, 62
  'Phoenix' 50, 62
  'Silver Vein' 50
Acer dasycarpum 48
Acer davidii 50, **50**, 62, 90
Acer douglasii 43
Acer x freemanii 47, 57, 90
  'Autumn Blaze' 47, **48**, 57, 90
  'Autumn Fantasy' 47, 57

'Marmo' 47
Acer ginnala 41, 87
  'Durand Dwarf' 41
Acer glabrum 43
Acer griseum 37, **37**, 87, 90
Acer japonicum 38, 43, 60, 61, 62, 71, 87
  'Aconitifolium' 8, **17**, 38, **39**, 43, **61**, 89, **92**
  'Green Cascade' 39, **39**, 61,**61**
  'Vitifolium' 39
Acer macrophyllum 48
Acer micranthum 40
Acer mono 40
Acer morrisonensis 51
Acer negundo 43, 45, 60, 92
  'Elegans' 44, 60
  'Flamingo' **43**, 44, 60, 92
  'Kelly's Gold' 44, 60, 92
  'Violaceum' 45, **45**, 60
Acer palmatum 1, **2**, 26, **27**, **54**, 58, 63, 71, 87, 89
  'Aka-shigitatsu-sawa' 32
  'Aratama' 19, 58, **58**
  'Asahi-zuru' 32, **32**
  'Beni-fushigi' 20, **21**
  'Beni-hime' 20, **58**, 59

'Beni-komachi' 7, **18**, 20, **20**, 21, 58, **59**, **84**, 89
'Beni-maiko' 21, 59, 89
'Beni-otake' 21, **21**, **56**, 57, 89, **90**
'Beni-schichihenge' 32, **33**, 59
'Bloodgood' 7, 21, **22**, 23, **62**, 57, 59
'Burgundy Lace' 22, 23
'Butterfly' 33
'Chishio' **22**, 59, **85**
'Coreanum' 27
'Fireglow' 22, **22**
'Goshiki-kotohime' 33
'Hagaromo' 26
'Higasayama' 33, **33**, 57
'Inazuma' **23**
'Kagero' 33, 57
'Kamagata' 27, 59, **86**, **89**
'Katsura' **18**, 27, 57, 89
'Koreanum' 27
'Kotohime' 27
'Koto-ito-komachi' 27
'Linearilobum' 27, **28**
'Linearilobum Rubrum' 27
'Lutescens' 28, 57, 89
'Okagami' **19**, 57, 89
'Omurayama' **28**, 29
'Orange Dream' 27

'Orido-nishiki' 7, 34
'Osakazuki' 29, 57
'Peaches and Cream' 34, **34**
'Pixie' 23, 59
'Red Pygmy' 23
'Roseomarginatm' 33
'Sango-kaku' **3**, 29
'Scolopendrifolium' 27
'Senkaki' 29
'Shaina' 23, **23**
'Sherwood Flame' 23
'Shigitatsu-sawa' 32, **32**, 57
'Shin-deshojo' 7, 23, **24**, 55, **56**, 80, 89, **92**
'Sumi-nagashi' **7**, 24
'Trombenburg' 24
'Ukigumo' 34
'Ukon' 29, **29**, 59
'Villa Taranto' 29, 57
Acer palmatum atropurpureum **16**, 19, **86**
'Moonfire' 20
'Okagami' **16**, 20
'Oshio-beni' 20
'Sumi-nagashi' 20
Acer palmatum var. *dissectum* **12**, 24, **30**, **31**, 58, **60**, **77**, 80, 85, 89
'Crimson Queen' 24, 25, **26**, **69**, **71**, **76**, **83**, 91
'Dissectum Atropurpureum' 25
'Ever Red' **14**, 25, **82**
'Filigree' 29, **31**, **77**
'Flavescens' 30
'Garnet' 25, **25**
'Ornatum Variegatum' 34, **34**
'Palmatifolium' 30
'Paucem' 30
'Red Dragon' 25, **25**
'Red Filigree Lace' 25
'Rubifolium' 25, **26**
'Seiryu' 30, **30**, 57, **91**
'Sekimori' 30
'Tamukayama' 25
'Toyama-nishiki' 34, **91**
'Viridis' 30, **30**
Acer palmatum var. *heptalobum* 27, **27**, 29, 57
Acer pensylvanicum 45, 60, 90
'Erythrocladum' 46

Acer pictum 40
Acer platanoides 51, **51**, 62, 90
'Crimson King' 7, **50**, 51, 62, 90
'Crimson Sentry' 51, 91
'Drummondii' 51, 62
Acer pseudoplatanus 51, 62, 91
'Brilliantissimum' 7, 52, **52**, 62, 91
'Esk Flamingo' 52, **52**, 62
'Esk Sunset' **49**, 52, **53**, 62, 91
'Leopoldii' 52
'Prince Handjery' 52
Acer rubrum 8, **45**, 46, 56, **60**, 87, 90
'Armstrong' **10**, 46
'Armstrong II' **42**, 46, 57
'Bowhall' 46, 57
'October Glory' 46, **46**, 57, **65**, 90
'Red Sunset' 46, **47**, 57
'Scanlon' 47, **47**, **57**
'Schlesingeri' 47, 57
Acer rubrum x *freemanii* 'Autumn Blaze' **93**
Acer rufinerve 41
'Albolimbatum' **36**, **40**, 41
'Winter Gold' 41
Acer saccharinum 48, 57, 90
'Bonfire' 48, 58, 92
'Born's Gracious' 48, 57
'Brocade' 48, 58
'Lutescens' 48, 57
'Newton Sentry' 48, 58
Acer shirasawanum 41
'Autumn Moon' **11**, **40**, 41, 91
'Full Moon' 41
Acer sieboldianum 41
Acer spicatum 48
Acer tataricum subsp. *ginnala* 41
aphids 15
ash-leaved maple 43
big-leaf maple 48
bonsai 86–87
box elder 43, 92
bulbs 77
Cappadocian maple 49
care 13
Caucasian maple 49
chlorosis 15
coliseum maple 49
companion planting 65–81
  bulbs 77–81

perennials 73–77
shrubs 68–73
trees 65–68
containers 83–86
cuttings 17
die-back 15
full-moon maple 38
grafting and budding 17
green selection 26
green weeping maples 29
hard maple 48
Hardiness Zone Map 9
harlequin maple 51
hedge maple 49
location 11
Manitoba maple 43
moosewood 45
mountain maple 48
Norway maple 51, 90
Oregon maple 48
paperbark maple 37
Père David's maple 50
perennials 73
pests and diseases 15
planetree maple 51
planting 12
propagation 16–17
  cuttings 17
  grafting and budding 17
  from seed 16
pruning 15
red maples 19, 46
red weeping maples 24
redvein maple 41
rock maple 48
root rot 15
scale 15
scarlet maple 46
shrubs 68
snakebark maple 8, 46, 51, 60
soil 11
striped maple 45
sugar maple 48, 57
sycamore maple 51
thunder maple 23
trident maple **13**, 37
variegated maples 30
verticillium wilt 15